The SHELF

Faith, PTSD, and Overcoming Me

David K. DeRemer

ISBN 978-1-64569-334-5 (paperback)
ISBN 978-1-64569-335-2 (digital)

Copyright © 2019 by David K. DeRemer

All rights reserved. No part of this publication may be reproduced, distributed, or transmitted in any form or by any means, including photocopying, recording, or other electronic or mechanical methods without the prior written permission of the publisher. For permission requests, solicit the publisher via the address below.

Christian Faith Publishing, Inc.
832 Park Avenue
Meadville, PA 16335
www.christianfaithpublishing.com

Printed in the United States of America

To my children, each a distinct and unique reflection of their father, each with their own world still yet to explore, bearers of unyielding faith and strength, who consistently inspire my heart so profoundly.

One day when you read my story, I pray it be a small window through which you understand your father, Jesus Christ, and the amazing world that awaits you!

CONTENTS

Preface 7
Acknowledgments 9
Introduction: Understanding "The Shelf" 11

Chapter 1	My Beginning on the Shelf	13
Chapter 2	My Worst Nightmare	19
Chapter 3	A Father Exposed	28
Chapter 4	Abuse	35
Chapter 5	My Solace	46
Chapter 6	The Reunion	52
Chapter 7	The Next Phase	58
Chapter 8	My Career, Part 1	64
Chapter 9	Misty and the Beginning of Parenthood	...71
Chapter 10	My Career, Part 2	79
Chapter 11	Bosnia	84
Chapter 12	My Career, Part 3	100
Chapter 13	My Girls	109
Chapter 14	Putting Misty on the Shelf	126
Chapter 15	Faith and Fasting	131
Chapter 16	Divorce and Bodybuilding	142
Chapter 17	Her	146
Chapter 18	Moving Mountains	157
Chapter 19	Saying Goodbye	169
Chapter 20	First Impressions	174

Chapter 21	Darkness	178
Chapter 22	Getting Help	185
Chapter 23	Baptism	188
Chapter 24	PTSD, Abandoholism, and Me	193
Chapter 25	Military Muscle	197
Chapter 26	The Calling	206
Chapter 27	Losing Purpose	215
Chapter 28	The Glorious Unfolding	221

Conclusion 229

PREFACE

We all have moments in life when we question our worth, those moments when significant events in life cause us to question everything we know, moments when we feel so beaten down and broken that we wonder what our purpose in life truly is—or if we even have one. It's easy to get bogged down in the mire of life and one day wake up and realize you don't know who you are anymore.

I've been through a lot. I don't profess to have lived through the worst things ever, but I've struggled, and I've suffered. My childhood wasn't great; I've been through a divorce; I've lost friends and family; and post-traumatic stress disorder has been a part of my life, which I'd lived with for many years without even knowing I suffered from it.

My form of PTSD stems from abandonment, one whose signs and symptoms are lesser known to most people. It's a condition triggered by trauma that affects a person in their current life and generally stems from childhood. That was the case for me. Imagine living forty years of your life with behavioral triggers inside you that you didn't even know existed.

Many suffer from this form of PTSD but don't realize it. The ones who do often live their lives being labeled by people unfairly, struggle with personal relationships and social situations, and are often regarded by others as being moody, extremely insecure, and needy.

I was that guy. Well, to be perfectly honest, I still am that guy. Of course, I have lived with PTSD since I was very young, so I imagine I always will be that guy. It wasn't until significant events in my adult life unfolded—and the triggers became too much—that it all became clear. This is the story I'm about to tell.

But it's also a story about faith, and a story that you'd likely have to live to ever believe. The stories you're about to read about how God has moved mountains in my life will have you screaming and crying and questioning everything you know. They'll have you wondering if it's truth or a fairy tale. At least, that's what it did for me, and I'm the one who lived it. It's very real; make no mistake about that.

My journey has been filled with many obstacles. I've been from one end of the spectrum to the other with regard to self-esteem, being happy, and forming real bonds and real relationships with people. Ultimately, for me, it was a tough pill to swallow when I looked back at my life and finally understood that more times than not, I was the problem, and that I was my own worst enemy.

My faith in God changed everything. And now, I'm here to share my story because it's what He called me to do. If parts of my story sound familiar to you already or resemble how you feel inside, the pages that follow may help you find your way; that's my hope at least. God can create so many miracles in your life if you just believe in Him, and you'll read about many of my own miracles here. I've seen His work firsthand, and it's magical.

ACKNOWLEDGMENTS

Thank you to my family and friends and to all the people at Christian Faith Publishing for their tireless efforts in helping me bring my story to life. I couldn't have asked for a better group of people to help me turn all of this into a reality in order to inspire, motivate, and help others turn their lives around like I did.

INTRODUCTION

Understanding "The Shelf"

We've all been placed on the shelf.

I'm sure most of you are sitting there thinking, *What is this shelf, and what does that mean?* Well, as I first sat on my couch thinking about writing this book and how I'd go about doing it, I had a vision. It was a vision of a room; and in this room, there was a bookcase and a table. As I thought more about my story and how to put my life and struggles into context so anyone could understand, that vision became clearer. And from that came the title of this book. It'll make sense as we go along.

You see, in my world, the "shelf" was the place your mother put you when she didn't want you. The shelf was the place your dad put you when you wanted him to play football with you, and he just told you to go outside and play. The shelf was the place your only best friend put you when he chose to betray your trust. And the shelf you may have put others on without even realizing it.

Maybe this "shelf" doesn't make a whole lot of sense to you. But think of it like this: Think of the things you have in your living room or in your office on a shelf: books, picture frames, maybe a souvenir from a trip you took ten years ago. These are all things that were once important enough for you to create, buy, own, have, or highlight, but now may just sit on a shelf—rarely used, talked about, or noticed. These are things that you still have and don't want to necessarily get rid of; however, they're things that no longer have enough significance in your life to be the centerpiece of your dining room table or the main source of conversation when entertaining friends. Make sense? This, my friends, is what I mean by the shelf.

We don't realize how often we are put on the shelf as people. We become so complacent in life that when we are put on the shelf, we don't even realize it until it's too late. If this is starting to make sense and sounds familiar to you, I hope that after you're done reading, you'll be fully equipped and motivated to change something in your life and never allow yourself to be put there again.

Life happens, and things change. How you're treated changes; how you're viewed changes. I'm certain everyone has experienced the shelf in some way, shape, or form. You'll hear me talk about it often in this book when I speak of my own experiences of being cast aside as just an option and never being made a priority. If you too were once the centerpiece of the dining room table—one your mother, father, friends, or significant other had pride in—but feel you now have just been relegated to a lonely spot on the shelf in the corner of a room that no one ever talks or cares about, then this book is for you. Hang on for the ride.

> It is the Lord who goes before you. He will be with you; he will not leave you or forsake you. Do not fear or be dismayed.
>
> —Deuteronomy 31:8

CHAPTER 1

My Beginning on the Shelf

My very first memory of being put on the shelf began with my mother. My parents divorced in 1980 when I was five years old, and it was just my three-year-old brother Mark and I back then—the only children my parents had together. Mark and I left home with my mother, bouncing around from school to school and home to home.

There were times when all we had to eat was stale bread and ketchup. There were times when the three of us slept in our car because we had no place else to go. Through my innocent young eyes, I guess I never understood the gravity of our situation or truly grasped how dire our circumstances were. Maybe I can attribute that to my mother as she likely sheltered us from a horrible situation the best way she knew how to at the time. I'd like to think that was the case, anyway. Regardless, I had no idea what was wrong or the reasons why they were wrong, I just knew that everything in our life had changed, and there was nothing I could do about it but just go along for the ride.

As I said, we bounced around from home to home. My mother got odd jobs as a waitress and doing whatever other jobs she could find. My brother and I had spent more time with babysitters than anyone else—babysitters who often left us alone and beat us. I remember trying to protect my brother so many times. I took more than my fair share of beatings for that. But even as a five-year old, I always had an instinct to take care of him and other people.

My dad would sometimes come and get us on the weekends during this time. I remember sitting so anxiously by the clock—the minutes feeling like days—waiting for five o'clock to come on those Fridays when it was "daddy's turn." He'd come get us, take us to the park, and to get ice cream at "Friendly's." There wasn't a stepmother in the picture yet as my father had set out to do his own thing—travel and see the world, I'd come to find out later (if that was even true).

I heard so many conflicting stories over the years about what caused my parents' divorce, my family history, and so many other things. I still don't really know a lot today about what's true and not true about my family tree, my heritage, or where I even came from. It's sad to have someone ask you about the origins of your last name and having no earthly idea other than what Google might tell you today. The only thing I ever heard was that there was a family history in Wales, or that the name was Welsh. That came from my father; and as it turned out, you could only believe about one percent of anything that ever came out of his mouth. Regardless, I was so happy to see him during those younger days. He was my idol, the perfect man who could do no wrong in my eyes, and I missed him every second that he was gone.

THE SHELF

The last place I remember living with my mother and brother before our circumstances became a little better (and our environment a little safer) was in the back part of this rather large home an older couple lived in. It gave us our own space with everything we needed despite being attached to the main home. I still remember days when I would take my brother around the outside of the entire house and set off all the mousetraps the owner had set. The owner was so mad when he found out.

I remember that place because of small things like that; but most importantly, because that's where I first started playing basketball. That's where I discovered that playing basketball was my getaway, and it would end up being that way for most of my life. It was always something I could do when I had so much on my mind that I couldn't get control of even as a small child. The world always seemed to just go away for a while when I had a basketball in my hands and a goal to shoot for— figuratively and literally. I spent many hours on that basketball goal, even at an age where I struggled to just barely get the ball to the rim.

(*Note*: If you're reading this, and you've shot around with me, or spent time with me on the court in a casual nongame way, congratulations. You were trusted and allowed to enter a sacred bubble that you probably never even knew existed. That didn't happen with just anyone because it was always my safe place, and not everyone felt safe to me all the time.)

This was the place we lived when my mother finally met the man who would end up becoming our stepfather and a very significant part of our lives. Michael was a hardworking man who put in many hours every day working for the local electric company. My mother met him at a small diner next door to where we lived—a place my brother and I would visit often with my mother when she could afford to take us. She worked there for a time, along with working at a bowling alley across the street from where we lived. It made things convenient for her, and better for us, being employed so close by, although we still never saw her much.

It wasn't her fault. She worked hard and did the best she could to provide for us and keep us safe. I missed her when she was gone. I remember leaving the house one day without the babysitter knowing and crossing the busy street to the bowling alley to see her. I guess getting my hair ripped out of my head and being beaten by the babysitter was just too much for me that day.

It wasn't until things got serious with my mother and Michael that I felt I was put on the shelf for the first time. My mother met him a year after her divorce to my father; and after dating for a time, Mom, Mark, and I ended up moving in with Michael. I don't remember much about the details or how it happened, of course, but I do remember feeling that he was not my father, and he would never be my father. That was a very significant problem for me. It would end up being a problem for my mother also.

As a young child, I guess I was just like any other child of divorce would be. Some children are more attached to one parent than the other. Looking back, that was my father for me. In no way, shape, or form could any man be him or take his place in my life. I remember missing him dearly as I tried to wrap my head around what was happening back then. The introduction of a new man into my daily routine wasn't just hard for me—I was just never going to allow it to happen.

Now let me just say this first: Michael wasn't a bad man. He worked hard and had his issues like anyone else. He was a Vietnam veteran and dealt with the daily struggles that most Vietnam veterans do. And now, as a retired military veteran myself, I understand his struggles better as an adult than I ever did as a small child.

Michael had a problem with alcohol and often isolated himself from the rest of us when he'd come home from work. It was his daily routine to get home, start drinking, and sit in the kitchen at the table watching television while the rest of us were in the living room or upstairs in our rooms. Looking back now, I understand why he was that way. My issues with him were not for any other reason than he just wasn't my daddy. I was young; I never let him in. I just want to make that clear. My issues being there were never about Michael, and despite his issues with alcohol, he never laid a hand on me, never treated me poorly, and ended up raising my brother to be the amazing man he is today.

I remember the conversation; it was your standard "you're not my daddy" type of thing, and he didn't like it. I'm not sure what prompted me to say that, but I'm sure it was my not wanting to do what I was told, or Michael's having as hard of a time adjusting as I was. The words and actions that followed would be the words and actions that ended up changing the entire course of my life, shaping me into who I am today. As a five-year-old, I was told, "If you don't like it, then go live with your father." And that's exactly what ended up happening. That's exactly what my mother allowed to happen. My very first experience with being put on the shelf.

As a musician, my father grew up playing in bands and had a multitude of musical talents, including playing the piano, playing the guitar, and singing. This is important to know at this point because my dad bought me a guitar prior to this all happening, and it was one of the only things I remember carrying around with me as my mom, brother, and I traveled from place to place. It was as big as I was, so I'm sure you can just picture this little kid lugging around (or more like dragging around) this huge guitar-shaped torn-up cardboard box that I kept the guitar in. No matter where we went, I always put that guitar back in the box and carried it to the next place time after time after time. Fast-forward to that day when those words were said by my stepfather and there I was, a very young boy with my bag of things and that worn-down cardboard guitar box by my side, sitting outside on the curb, waiting for my daddy to come pick me up for good.

My mother put me on the shelf. She chose her new man and new life over me and sent me on my way. As that very young child, she sent me away from her, away from my brother, away from everything comfortable that I had ever known in my life. Life wasn't always good or easy, but we did it together—the three of us. And suddenly, that was changing. I wasn't a priority for her then, and there were many years that followed when I questioned if I ever was.

> For my father and my mother have forsaken
> me, but the Lord will take me in.
>
> —Psalm 27:10

CHAPTER 2

My Worst Nightmare

Life with my father included a new stepmother, who married my father about a year after he swooped me up off that worn-down curb and loaded me and that falling-apart cardboard guitar box into the trunk of his car. Along with a new stepmother came a new stepsister, one whom I always had trouble getting along with. It never really felt good or comfortable for me; but at the time, I was young and didn't care about anything other than the fact that I had my daddy—my role model—and he was enough.

As I remember them, the couple of years that followed were somewhat normal. My father was a professional bass fisherman at the same time as being an insurance salesman, so I remember those early years of my life spending some weekends on the water with him in one of his two bass boats. We'd always have contests to see who could catch the most fish. I'd sit in the back of the boat in my life jacket catching tiny perch and crappie, while he'd haul in five-pound smallmouth bass from under docks, lily pads and cattail-covered bays.

I was so enamored by him, the things he could do and how he seemed to just be the very best at everything. He would win fishing tournaments all the time. He could play the guitar and the piano. He was salesman of the month and salesman of the year for more years than I could count, as the obscene amount of plaques covering his home office walls could attest. He could do no wrong in my eyes, and I looked up to him more than anyone. In my young eyes at the time, he was just the perfect dad.

Because he was self-employed, my father was always home in the mornings before he'd go off to work. During the summer, I always loved that because I would get to see him more. My stepmother and I didn't get along all that well right from the start, but at this point, she still had a normal job and was gone early in the morning and didn't return home until the early evening. So it would just be me, my father, and my stepsister at home all day during the summer.

I always loved Mondays because my father was home all day, as that was the day he would call clients and schedule appointments for the rest of the week. He always had a home office, so he did it all from home. In fact, for a long time until we moved into a bigger home, my bedroom was in his office. We lived in a three-bedroom trailer; and since my stepsister was older, she got the other room to herself. That room and my parents' bedroom were on one end of the trailer, and my room was on the opposite end with the living room and kitchen in between.

I had a couch that turned into a horribly uncomfortable fold-out bed to sleep on, a single white dresser, and an old black-and-white television that, if you turned the rabbit ears antenna just right, you could hear a channel or two. Yes, I said *hear* a channel or two; I was lucky to ever get a picture. It was modest living at best for the 1980s, but it was what I had. I never really had much; no room for posters on the walls then, no room for photos of my brother or anything personal. The walls of my "room" were covered with plaques my dad had earned in his business and memorabilia of his own. I guess I never really thought much about it then; it was the only life I really knew, and I was just living it.

As I said, summers were the best time of year for me as I got to see my father more and spend more time with him. As a child, I was never really a priority for him, but any time I had with him was perfect in my eyes. I grew up fast, so it wasn't long until I knew otherwise. It may have seemed perfect, but I was really just a burden whom he had to play with once in a while. "Perfection" was never really the case; however, after being cast aside by my mother a year or two before, any attention felt good whether intentional or not.

I was always awake before everyone else in my house; and more times than not, I'd be dressed and out the door to see what havoc I could cause in the quiet neighborhood just as the bright sun would come up. I was an active and curious child, which had often caused turmoil for my parents—and likely why I always seemed to be in trouble or grounded. However, I was also a very intelligent and incredibly observant child and always had the ability to read people, discover things, and truly find the "pulse" in any situation. It's a gift I still feel I have today and one that I feel has helped me become a good mentor to all the people who have worked for me.

The summer morning that changed my life still isn't an easy one to talk about. There were so many times while writing the first manuscript for this book that I didn't even want to include this part of my life. But after years of struggle and extensive counseling for severe anxiety and depression, I discovered that abandonment shaped me into who I am, and it impacted my relationships; and the suppressed, major childhood traumas in my life, like this one, ended up playing a significant role in creating my lifelong struggles. So it's a part of me that can't be just discarded or left out of my story. This was the day that sent me into a downward spiral I never realized was happening until almost thirty years later.

I woke up early that summer day just like any other summer morning. I was excited about starting the day. I remember the sun, just starting to come up over the colorful mountains in the horizon, shining bright into my bedroom window and reflecting off my dad's gun cabinet's glass doors like it always did. It was quiet in the house, so I knew I was the only one awake at the time.

As I said, I was always a very curious child; and along with that, I was also a little prankster with an enormous sense of humor. As much as my stepsister and I didn't get along, I must admit to the fact that most of our sibling angst was likely my fault. I taunted her, made fun of her, and played pranks on her all the time. I was small in stature as a child, and she was always much bigger than me, so I was able to run faster and get away from her most of the time when she'd get angry. Sometimes she'd catch me though—and Lord help me, I got my butt kicked often. I deserved it, though, I guess. Either way, on this particular morning, I guess I was feeling brave because I was up to no good. At the very least, I was going to at least sneak down to my sister's bedroom and scare the crap out of her and hope I didn't wake up my father when I did.

Out my bedroom door I went, skipping across the large living room and the worn yellow carpet beneath my sock feet. I continued, sliding in my socks through the kitchen like Tom Cruise and into the dining room, finally making it to the beginning of the long hallway undetected. My sister's room was the first door on the left about halfway down the hall, while my parents' bedroom was straight ahead at the end of the hall. We lived in a trailer, so you heard just about every creak and crack in the hollow floor with just about every step you took. However, over time, I had mastered the art of dodging the spots in the floor that made the most noise—you know, to maximize the impact of my normal sneak attacks on my sister or to locate and secure Snickers bars and Oreos I wasn't allowed to have…undetected.

I can imagine I looked like I was playing hopscotch as I made my way down the hallway to my sister's bedroom door. I remember this spot in front of her door being particularly tricky as there was only a tiny spot where you could step inside her doorway that didn't make noise. So I moved carefully, I moved slowly, and I always scoped out the situation prior to launching my attack. I moved just inside the door and peeked around the wall to her bed just to see how she was positioned and figure out what I was going to do next. What I discovered was a surprise: she wasn't there.

Remember, I'm probably around seven years old at that time. I was young and innocent and naive, but incredibly smart and observant; and after all I had already been through in my life up to that point, I had a pretty good grasp on the real world and things I probably shouldn't have at the time.

I stood in her doorway surprised, but immediately thought that maybe she had just gone to work with her mother that morning. At seven years old, your mind isn't so negatively conditioned to the real world that you immediately think of something bad or something negative when you first discover something out of the ordinary. I imagine if you had seen me in that moment, I probably just sort of shrugged my shoulders, as I likely thought *oh well* to myself and just decided to save my "attack" for another time.

With all that in mind, I decided to just continue my trek down the hallway to my father's bedroom and just peek in on him to see if he was awake yet, like I did sometimes. I would often make him coffee and take it down to his bedroom so he'd have it when he woke up. I didn't really do it for him, though; I did it so it would wake him up, and I could spend more time with him. I'd always slide the coaster on his nightstand over toward him, knowing it made noise and would wake him. I wasn't dumb; he was my hero, and I wanted every second with him that I could get.

That morning was different, though. It was a running joke in our house that my father snored so loud that he'd peel paint off the walls. On those mornings when I'd take coffee down to his bedroom, I'd always know it was safe to make the "run" down the noisy hallway during those long loud snores. I'd patiently wait for one to come and *boom*, off I'd go. It was like that scene in *The Shawshank Redemption* when Andy is pounding the sewer pipe with a rock. Andy would wait until the thunder roared outside before he would strike the pipe with the rock in order to mask the sound. I employed that same strategy during the snores. Every time he snored, I moved. I was an expert at getting where I needed to go undetected.

But on this day, as I stood in silence in the doorway of my sister's bedroom, that was all I heard—silence. It was as if life had stopped. There was no snoring on this day, and I'll never forget standing there thinking that there wasn't. Again, I was very observant and had an incredible memory. Maybe my father and stepsister had gotten up before me and went somewhere? Maybe something was going on that morning that I didn't know about? Maybe they thought they'd all be back before I got up? I didn't know. I stood there for what seemed like forever before finally deciding to continue down the hallway to see for myself if everyone was in fact gone. It was at this point that my carefree, seven-year-old "oh well" attitude turned into caution, a feeling of having to protect myself, and fear. I was still naive to the world to ever imagine what I was about to see; but in that moment, I remember being overcome with a darkness like I had never felt before.

I continued down the hallway. One very slow and careful step after another. It was dead silent, but even my carefully planned steps to the places in the floor that I knew wouldn't make a sound, sounded to me in that moment like a wrecking ball crashing into a large building. Suddenly, every single sound—every single breath I took, every heartbeat—seemed magnified by ridiculous proportions in my mind. Reality was, not a single sound was being made. And suddenly, without even knowing why, I was really scared.

I remember taking that final step and making it to the doorway of my father's bedroom, my young legs trembling and in pain after so cautiously taking so many steps on my tiptoes so as not to make any noise. I leaned around the corner, but because of the nightstand and lamp that were right inside the doorway and because of my height at the time, I couldn't see the bed from where I was standing. My father slept on the side of the bed closest to the door, but my view only allowed me to see the top of the lamp; if I moved in any further, he'd see me. I needed to move or duck down under the lampshade to see if my father was still there or still asleep. Instead, I stood on my tiptoes and peered over the top of the lamp. Of course, all that did was allow me to see the other side of the bed where my father wasn't.

What I was able to see, though, caused a confusion in me like I'd never experienced before. At the footboard end of that side of the bed lay my sister's pajamas she'd been wearing the night before. At seven years old, it still didn't make sense at this point. Why were those there?

I'll never forget that moment as the image has become a permanently burned image in my head that I can still see today almost forty years later. The pajamas were more of a nightgown she slipped over her head and went all the way to her feet. On the front was a cartoon of a little girl next to an open window and a big plate of butter flying out of the window. At the top, it read, "Why did the girl throw the butter out the window?" At the bottom, it read, "Because she wanted to see a butterfly." I'll never forget it. And as I saw them, I could feel tears welling up in my eyes. Again, after all I had been through in my life in my seven years, I wasn't completely naive and probably knew much more about some adult topics than I should have. In that instant, I grew up fast. In that instant, I suddenly knew what I was about to see.

It seemed like forever, but I'm sure it was only mere seconds between seeing those pajamas on the bed and positioning myself to finally be able to see my father lying naked on his back with my naked stepsister lying on top of him. I'm sure shock set in as all I could think about in that moment was ensuring I found every single quiet spot in the hallway floor to make it back to my bedroom without being detected. That trip felt like it took forever, but I finally made it. I walked back through the kitchen and dining room and into the living room with tears in my eyes and the start of uncontrollable crying. I stopped in the living room because there was a photo of my stepmom sitting on the speaker in the living room, and I couldn't stop staring at it. I just kept saying out loud, "Why aren't you here?"

I felt alone, confused, and above all, betrayed. Here was a man that I looked up to and wanted to be like lying in bed naked with a child. I was smart enough to know what that meant and how completely wrong it was. She was only a couple years older than me at the time—a child. He took advantage of her; he stole her childhood from her. As a very young child, I knew in my heart in that moment that he was nothing like the man I wanted to be, nothing like anything I ever wanted to be like, nothing I wanted to even be around anymore. To have your world turned upside down in an instant is excruciating at that age. To have the whole world as you know it shattered right before your very eyes is awful. My role model wasn't a role model at all. He was nothing more than a sick fake who cared about only himself and his own personal gratification and satisfaction. And to make matters worse, there was nothing I could do about it. I couldn't say a word.

He destroyed my childhood and any innocence I had left. Suddenly, I had no one to look up to, no one to be like, and no one to confide in. All trust was gone; I had nothing. It felt as if I had been gutted of any good I had left in me. Again, I felt like I was put on the shelf and forgotten about. That's how I felt from that moment on: helpless, hopeless, alone, trapped. It's sad to feel that way as a young child. What's worse is being that young and feeling like the only thing you can do is just bottle it all up, tuck it away, and never talk about it—ever—to anyone. And that's exactly what happened.

I wish I could say that was the last time I ever knew of things like this happening between my father and my stepsister, but it's a nonfiction book, and I unfortunately can't make up the story line as I go. My stepmother would attend ceramics classes on Wednesday nights, giving my father a prime opportunity to visit my stepsister in her room at night on a weekly basis in addition to many other times during the summers. I can't honestly say I saw with my own eyes what was happening in her room during those times, but seeing what I did see that morning was enough for me to know for sure.

He went there like clockwork not just on those Wednesdays but whenever he had the opportunity. I remember always going to bed and then a few minutes later camping out in the doorway of my room, peeking out at my father in his living room chair, and waiting for him to get up and walk down the hallway to her room whenever my stepmother was gone. It became such a regular occurrence that I

THE SHELF

could almost time it perfectly as to when I'd get to my bedroom door to peer out and when he'd get up to go to her room. I can still clearly see in my head the images of him in his chair and getting up to walk down there. It still sickens me today.

I almost got caught one night as he first walked to my room, flipped on the light, and asked if I was awake. When I pretended to be asleep and snoring, he flipped off the light and proceeded to my sister's room. I can still hear the very distinct sounds the walls and floor of her bedroom made when he finally made it to her room and walked in there. (Remember, I was a ninja at avoiding all those sounds when I'd walk down there. He, apparently, was not.)

As horrible as it all is, I think I was just numb to all of it at that point. Of course, I'd find out later that it was just shock, and that I had just tucked it all away for more than thirty years. Either way, when you're trapped and feel you're in a position where there's nothing you can do, and no one would believe you, it just makes you numb. Or maybe I was just too young to know how to handle it. I still don't really know; numb is the only word I can think of now that comes close to maybe describing how it all made me feel and why I just tucked it away for so long.

My father put me on the shelf. I wasn't a priority for him like a child should be to a parent—like my children are to me today. I wasn't a son he cared about and wanted to set an example for; I was just an option to have around. I was his reason to not pay extra child support to my mother. I was nothing to him. I want to get angry about it even today, but I can't. I think I'm still numb today like I was that day, numb that my father would do that, numb that any person could do that., numb that I still have to live with it.

> Fear not, for I am with you;
> be not dismayed, for I am your God;
> I will strengthen you, I will help you,
> I will uphold you with my righteous right hand.
>
> —Isaiah 41:10

CHAPTER 3

A Father Exposed

The thought of hugging or loving my father after that was repulsive to me. I didn't want him to touch me, I didn't want to be around him, and I certainly couldn't look at him or my stepsister the same way again after that. At that time, it wasn't my stepsister's fault. I didn't look at her with animosity or anger; it was just hard to look at her as a child like me and imagine the type of things that were likely going on inside of her. I wanted to talk to her about it so many times but just couldn't muster the courage at that age, I guess.

Regardless, even as a young child, I knew how to put on a fake smile and play the game; and in that situation, I had no choice but to do so. I just had to act like everything was okay. That's what I knew. That's what I felt was my only option at the time. I didn't feel like I could tell anyone, so I didn't. It made me so sick living like that for so many years. I felt trapped, but I was all alone with no way out, so life just went on.

As I said, those sorts of things continued to happen; and because I was so numb to it, I guess maybe I just stopped caring, looking, or worrying about it. I tried so many times to talk to my stepsister about it, as I said, because there was a concerned side of me even then that was worried about her, but I never said anything. The closest I ever got to saying something was one night while we were doing dishes. She'd always wash the dishes, and I'd always dry them and set them on the table for my stepmother to "check" before I could put them away (think Cinderella and wicked stepmother). I simply told my stepsister, "I know something you don't." I think she may have asked what just once and then told me to shut up or something like that. I'm not sure why I put it that way—maybe I just wanted her to pry it out of me; I don't know. After that, though, I just suppressed it along with everything else that had happened in my life and went on my way. However, it wouldn't be long before it would all come out, and the events I had witnessed would become front and center in our lives and change everything as I knew it—and not in a way that I or any of you would ever have expected it to.

Because my father had been so successful in his job, he and my stepmother would often go on vacations and trips all over the world. I remember them going to places like the Virgin Islands, London, and other amazing places like that. These weren't day trips to the spa either; they were vacations to luxurious resorts, islands, and countries that lasted a week or more.

I remember being shipped off to any family member or friend who would take me during those times, and they happened often. Some people I knew, some I didn't. It seems like the story of my life, looking back now: being shipped off and passed around to various people like a car or a lawn mower they were borrowing for a little while. Sometimes, even the people whom I was shipped off to would ship me off to someone else! Never once did I ever feel like I truly knew what home or real family was while living there.

I'm not sure what trip it was my father and stepmother went on this time or how it all played out in the days prior to their leaving. What I am sure of is that while they were gone on this trip, I was staying with a neighbor who lived two trailers down from us. My stepsister was staying in our house with her uncle (the brother of my stepmother) and his girlfriend. Looking back now, it doesn't really make sense as to why I would stay in a house about fifty feet away, but I do remember something being said about its being better for my stepsister and me because we didn't get along. Plus, being in an environment with her and her uncle—who both made fun of me and threw me around at every opportunity—didn't appeal to me all that much anyway.

The neighbors, Barb and Donnie, were always nice to me. I often went to their house to see them when none of my friends were available to play. They had a baby, and I always remember playing with her and just feeling like it was nice to have people care about me. Barb was more caring and nurturing to me than my stepmother was, so I was very okay with being there. In fact, I was excited that I was going to be staying there.

My parents left for their trip, and I spent my week truly enjoying my time with the neighbors. I tried not to pay much attention to what was going on at home and don't think I even went there much at all that week, except for maybe once to get a shirt or something. Apparently, there was a lot going on there during that time—things that my stepsister was doing with the adults that she wasn't supposed to be doing. Drinking and smoking cigarettes, as I remember it. I don't remember all the details of how everything went down when my parents returned home, but I do remember a lot of that coming out, along with my uncle being kicked out by my father because he drove my father's car while they were gone after being told he was not allowed to do so.

At this point, things were completely blowing up. I remember knowing that my parents were home, but I still stayed with the neighbors for a couple more nights after that. I didn't understand why, but at that age and with all the fun I was having, I wasn't going to question it. I was having fun. My childhood was not fun. My stepmother was a cross between the wicked stepmother in *Cinderella* and Judge Judy—literally. Add in some "you're worthless and won't ever amount to anything" comments (expletives excluded) and my being slapped, scratched, and beaten with her bare fists regularly (or anything she could get her hands on), and that was my life at home from age five to age sixteen or so. I say all that at this point to truly help you understand how happy I was to not have to go home right away when they returned from their trip. I hated home; I never felt like I ever was "home" for most of my life.

When I finally did go home, I was almost immediately summoned to the living room where I was told to sit in one of the chairs. My father was in his chair, and my stepmother was on the opposite side of the room in her chair. The atmosphere was so serious. My stepsister was nowhere to be found. As I sat there, I just remember thinking, *I didn't do it!*

THE SHELF

My stepmother told me we needed to have a serious conversation, and that I need to make sure I told the truth. She then proceeded to ask me—in very general terms—if I had seen anything happen with regard to my father and my stepsister. I'm not sure how I ever got involved or why anyone would ever think that I had seen something. But they thought it, and they asked.

I hadn't said a word to anyone about what I saw that morning or the things I had seen after that. Regardless, I proceeded to tell her the truth. I don't remember exactly how it was received by her as my nervous little hazel eyes were totally fixated on my father, sitting ever so smugly in his chair, confident that he would be able to weasel his way out of this one like he had likely done so many other times before. And that's exactly what happened. The next words I heard in an arrogant tone were, "Well, things aren't always as they appear."

Yes, that happened. That was all he had to say. I don't remember everything that was said, but those are the words I remember him saying repeatedly. I can still picture it and hear it even today. He couldn't even own up to any of it and never would, as there was no way anyone could ever prove it, and he knew it. And who was going to believe me?

You see, what had happened when my parents returned from that trip was that my stepsister either got caught drinking or smoking, and my parents found out somehow. And during my parents' finding out and punishing her, my stepsister got upset and told her mother about what my father had done to her. Of course, my stepmother was hesitant to believe it all when she heard it because it appeared that my stepsister was only saying it to deflect the attention off what she had done wrong.

The next day, I believe, I ended up going with my stepmother to her parents' house, as that's where they ended up taking my stepsister when all of this started to come out. I guess I was sort of sequestered away from what everyone was talking about as I only remember watching television and hanging out there until we left. The house was literally in the middle of a cornfield on the outskirts of a town, miles away from where we lived, and the driveway was about a mile long from the main road—literally. I say this because it was on that mile-long drive from the house to the main road that my stepmother and I had a very serious conversation when we left later that day.

She asked me if I had really seen something happen. Crying, I told her I had. I described it all in further detail and ensured her (as best as any child could) that everything I said was the truth. I also remember her asking me why I was crying, and I responded that I didn't want her to leave me. I didn't like her; but in that moment, I knew she had to be hurting too, right? It was her daughter! She was going to leave my father and who knew what would happen to me. I felt for her. I didn't want any of it to be true, and I didn't like telling her; but it was true, and I had to.

That drive down the long driveway to the main road seemed like forever. Life wasn't fun for me anyway; but in that moment, everything I knew was falling apart. My father, whom I looked up to and idolized, had betrayed me; my stepsister was gone; and now my stepmother was going to leave too. I felt for both my stepmom and stepsister, despite not liking them very much. And I felt nothing for my father at that moment.

Now that it was out, I had no idea what was going to happen next. What will happen to my father now? Will I get shipped back to my mother who doesn't want me? As we drove down that bumpy driveway surrounded by tall dried-out cornstalks, I had no idea what the next day was going to bring or where I would end up. Yet what ended up happening after that is beyond anything you could possibly comprehend or ever make okay in your mind. Did my stepmother leave my father? No. Did anything ever happen to my father? No. Did my stepmother stay married to my father? Yes. Are they still married today? Yes.

Amazing to think of, when you think of the magnitude of these horrible things happening and the negative impact it would have on so many. But instead of what would likely happen in most cases like this (jail time and divorce, I would imagine for normal people), my father and stepmother had an entirely different way to deal with it. Arrangements were made to rent a trailer so my stepsister could live there, while my stepmother lived with us and would just go back and forth. The other place was about twenty miles away from our home. Yes, that really happened.

THE SHELF

As it turned out, one of my stepmother's brothers also stayed there, and my stepmother spent the evenings there and traveled back and forth from that place to our house daily. This just caused even more chaos in my life as I couldn't be left alone at my own home when my father was working, so I ended up having to stay at my stepsister's new house most nights too. It caused all sorts of issues for me mentally and emotionally as I didn't like being there and spent most days struggling to just be comfortable in my own skin. All I wanted in my life was to just smile and be happy like a normal child was supposed to. But I couldn't; I just couldn't. I was never able to, not like that, not after all I had seen.

Later in life as an adult, I tried to have a relationship with my father. I knew I had to confront him and find some sort of resolution to this in order to have closure and be able to move past all the horrible things I had seen. I couldn't confront him for the longest time and just acted like things were fine during the couple times I went to New York to visit family.

The breaking point came when I took my daughters to New York to visit one summer. It was the first time I had been home with all three girls; and at the time, my oldest was about the same age as my stepsister was when all the bad things started happening. I had a very difficult time with my father being around my daughters. I never left them alone with him, and it truly got to the point where I couldn't stand being there anymore. I was very uncomfortable. He tried to take my daughter home by himself when she was sick one day, and we were all at my stepsister's house (yes, they were all very close long after I was gone). The thought of him being alone with her made me severely ill. I told him she was staying with me. He kept saying he was taking her; I kept saying she was staying with me. I felt sick; I felt angry. It was then that I knew this problem was bigger than I had ever imagined. I just couldn't get the past out of my mind, and now it was affecting me with my own children. So I did what any decent, protective father would do who felt the way I did. I gathered up my girls, left New York that summer, and never took them back there again.

I ended up confronting my father some years later in an e-mail, not getting too specific, but alluding to the past in a way that I knew he would understand. There was no mistaking what I was talking about. He responded with a very long e-mail talking about how "they" had all gotten over the past, and that I needed to just "get over it" also. You see, my father, stepmother, and stepsister had suddenly become one big happy family as adults. The whole situation was very strange and sick to me, considering what I knew, what I had seen repeatedly over the years, and the struggles I still had with it all myself ten, twenty, and even thirty years later.

To make matters worse, my stepsister had three daughters of her own—daughters that my father would babysit, help raise, and often be alone with. It made me sick to my stomach to think of that situation. Thoughts I had about their safety and well-being made me even more sick to my stomach. And the fact that my stepmother and stepsister would still be there, let alone allow those girls to be around him, continues to sicken me even to this day.

They wanted me to just "get over it." I couldn't; I still haven't. It certainly takes special kind of people to live a life the way they've lived it since those horrible things happened forty years ago. And I don't mean "special" in a good way; I mean, the kind of people you never want to be around or associate yourself with ever again. My stepmother once told me, "I've been through so much shit with your father that I'm not leaving no matter what. I'm gonna get mine." Apparently, she meant she was going to "get hers" at all costs. I think that kind of says it all about what kind of people they all were.

Regardless, I finally realized I had to just let go. I severed the relationship I had with all of them, and it has been years since I've spoken to any of them. Thankfully, I've been able to forgive, but I will never be able to forget.

> Let all bitterness and wrath and anger and clamor and slander be put away from you, along with all malice.
>
> —Ephesians 4:31

CHAPTER 4

Abuse

As if being mentally and emotionally destroyed before reaching age ten wasn't enough, I was physically abused too. Now I'm not going to sit here and say that I had it worse than anyone else because I know there are many stories out there—both told and untold—of abuse much worse than any I endured. Honestly, the physical abuse was the least of it as the residual effects of the mental and emotional torture I went through was what lingered on through the rest of my childhood years, and then into my adult life.

The physical abuse still wasn't good, however. My stepmother had quite a temper and, even with normal kid things, would react in a way that was always excessive. I remember one day getting caught putting sugar on my cereal and getting pounded on for what seemed like an hour. I was standing at the counter, and she just came up behind me and started punching and slapping me in the head, neck, shoulders, and back—just pounding and pounding as hard as she could, and all I could do was put my hands over my face and wait for it to end.

That's generally how it was every time it happened. It was like she completely went crazy for a full thirty to sixty seconds—a rage like I had never seen. And it's not like it was over being called a "bitch" to her face or over something extremely bad that would understandably produce that sort of rage; it was always over something small, the types of things I would generally just raise an eyebrow about to my own daughters if they had done it, or things that I might just shake my head and say "please don't do that again" about. But this was my norm. It continued well into my teen years until I ultimately ended up leaving my father's home and reuniting with my mother in the middle of my junior year of high school. You'll read more about that later on.

There was a significant amount of concern for me at school. Teachers, administrators, principals, and other prominent figures in my school system through the years must have had an idea of what was happening to me. Looking back, they always showed concern, asked me if I was okay, and tried to make things easier for me. I wasn't the best-acting student as I was always very hyper and outgoing. I even had to go see the principal once for something and ended up crying in his lap as he could see there was much more going on in my life than just what they could all see in school. The conversation turned from what I had done to what was being done to me at home.

THE SHELF

It seemed that there was a common understanding amongst all the adult figures in my life at school that I was struggling at home for some reason even if they didn't know what that reason was. I think that's what always made school a safe place for me. I was probably the only kid in school who dreaded Fridays and couldn't wait until Mondays. I was probably the only kid who hated snow days, winter and spring breaks, holidays, and summers. School was my safe place away from a world at home that had done nothing but hurt me.

I remember one day during gym class, I was walking on the grass on the inside of the track and being approached by my gym teacher. His name was Tom LaDuke. He was an imposing figure to me back then. He was the wrestling coach; he was the football coach; he was the coach of the city's semiprofessional football team. Everyone in the state knew who he was. To me, he always appeared to be seven feet tall and huge; he intimidated me.

I had a bad habit of forgetting my gym clothes and always needed to borrow some. I feared going into his office and asking him to do so as I knew he'd be mad, and I knew there would be push-ups or some other form of "payment" required for me to get them. He was never mad though, I know that now. He was just teaching me about responsibility and about accountability. He was an imposing figure, but also a caring man who had a lasting impression on me that I still carry to this day.

As he approached me on the track that day, he asked me what was wrong with my legs. It was an unusual question to ask as I was always an athlete, had always done well in gym class, and never had any issues running or doing whatever it was he had us do. I'm sure I responded with a confused look, but then he put his hand—which to me, appeared to be about the size of a telephone book—on my left shoulder and stopped me from walking. He then looked down at me and asked me if I was okay. Still confused, I told him I was and asked why. He then said, "Those are some pretty good bruises on your legs." I looked down in horror as bruises from a beating I had taken from my stepmother a day or two before were starting to form on my legs. There were three or four long dark, deep-purple bruises protruding from the bottom of my shorts and extending down to near the back of my knee on both legs. Most of my beatings could be hidden; some would bruise and some wouldn't. The stick she used this time was one she made me go get from the woods behind our house for her to use on me. I remember its being a good inch or so around. If I knew then what I know now, I probably wouldn't have gotten such a big stick for her to use—especially since she told me before I went out there what I was getting it for. Eh, live and learn.

I tried to play off the coach's comments. I don't remember specifically what I said, but I do remember tears welling up in my eyes and trying to hide it. I joked that my stepmom just had a hard time hitting her target or something like that. Again, I was trying to hide it. That didn't work out well as he noticed my tears, and the hand on my shoulder turned into a big hug.

I don't know if he ever said anything to anyone after that or if my parents were ever contacted. All I knew was, in that moment, someone cared about me—and that was something I was never used to. I think this was when I began to slowly understand that what was happening to me at home wasn't normal, and that being put on a shelf the way I was wasn't how life was really supposed to be for me. I'm sure the coach never knew the impact that moment made on me. Teachers are just amazing that way, I've learned. Mine were no different.

That wasn't the only way I would be punished for things. I wasn't the perfect kid, but I wasn't awful either. I never swore at my step-mom or dad. I rolled my eyes and was a smart mouth sometimes like any other kid, but I wasn't bad. But during those times when I would be a smart mouth, the punishments never seemed to fit the "crime." In addition to being talked down to and beaten, I often had my mouth forced open and had dish detergent poured down my throat. One time, my step-mom used a cheese grater to shred an *entire* bar of Dial soap and filled a cereal bowl with it and forced me to eat it. I couldn't do anything or go anywhere until I ate the entire thing. And they made me sit right in front of them with it, so they knew I did.

I was in so much pain after that. My tongue and throat were raw and bleeding for days. But much like was the case with everything

THE SHELF

else, I never told anyone. I never heard of any of my other friends ever having to do that—and in my mind, I didn't want anyone else to know because I simply was *not* going to be known as the "freak" who was forced to eat soap at home.

At this point, my self-esteem was almost nonexistent. It was hard to bottle up things and just put on a happy face every day at school like I was used to doing. It wasn't fair. I spent most of my life with few friends as I spent most of my days cleaning our house or grounded because one of my grades wasn't what my parents thought it should be. Grounded in our house meant that you stayed in your room with no television, no radio, and didn't come out of your room except to eat. It was like being in prison, and it lasted until the next report card came out regardless of any progress reports that may show improvement. I was a good student, and it didn't happen much because of grades, but it was brutal and cruel. All this on top of being beaten daily. I spent most of my days grounded for various reasons. It was a personal prison living at home for many reasons. Thus, I loved going to school so much; it was the only time I ever really saw anything other than the ceiling of my bedroom.

I was very restricted and never got to do much growing up. Looking back now, I realize that it was because my parents were selfish and just didn't want to take me anywhere or be a part of anything I was doing or wanted to do in my life. My dad spent hours playing video games when he wasn't at work, and my stepmother was busy running two households and catering to my father's every need and desire. My welfare wasn't really a part of their life, as I seemed to just be a burden they had to deal with every day.

I played on the school basketball team, and that was about it, but my parents never showed up to games to support me or cheer for me. Most of the time on game nights, long after my teammates and their parents and all the fans and coaches had left for home, I'd be the only one left at the school. On weekends for practices, if I was even able to go, I'd be the only one there for hours after it was over, waiting for a ride. (I did get to know the janitors well though.) If we had an away game, more times than not, I'd be the only kid there without a parent watching. I'd then end up riding the bus back to our school, and only the janitor and I would be there again as I waited for one of my parents or someone to decide to come pick me up.

I didn't know any better about any of that at the time; it just was my "normal." It really wasn't until I had my own kids—and never wanted to miss any of their games—that I realized how significant my parents' absence in my life really was. I've cried real tears and have felt so completely gutted on days when my military schedule or a deployment kept me from attending games and events for my kids. I can't imagine my girls ever feeling about me the way I feel about my father. I had no support or encouragement for anything. It kills me to think of ever being that way with my own children.

Not only did my parents never attend games or support me, there was a year or two when they made me quit playing on the basketball team completely. I'm not sure if it was just because they knew it was something I loved and wanted to take that away from me like everything else, or if they just got tired of having to take me to and from practices or go pick me up and be inconvenienced in some way. My grades sometimes slipped a little, and I remember that being the justification (this time) for making me quit during one of my J.V. years. I was completely devastated and struggled so much with being forced to quit and come home every day to a place I didn't want to be. I cried for hours every day, always wishing I was somewhere else. Wishing I was at practice. Staring at the game schedule while lying in my bed wishing I was where my team was. It was brutal.

This season was one I remember, not so much because my parents made me quit the team, but because of what happened after I quit. I was in my room, grounded as usual, and it was nearing Christmas. I think we were on Christmas vacation at the time, which was horrible for me because I spent the entire time in my room with no TV, no radio, no friends, no nothing. I already mentioned what "grounded" was like in my house. So, with that being the case, I often looked for any "excitement" that I could to make the dreadful minutes, that seemed like hours, go by faster—and when someone showed up at the house, it was something different to be curious about.

It was always the little things that kept me going.

THE SHELF

There was a knock at the door, and I went running to the doorway of my bedroom with my head stuck down the hallway as far as I could to see and hear what was going on. Of course, my room was too far away to see or hear anything, so when I heard the front door shut, I jumped back into my bed just in case my step-mom or dad came down the hallway. [Yes, I would've gotten yelled at if I got caught simply sticking my head out of my bedroom door too].

As it turned out, the person at the door was my basketball coach, Tedd Jamieson. Despite me no longer being on the team, he had come to give me a Christmas present. I never knew what sort of conversation my dad had with Mr. J at the time, but dad did end up coming into my room, throwing the gift down on me as I laid in my bed, and said to me in a snide tone, "it's from your coach." Then he just walked out.

As I sit here even now, almost 30 years later, I get emotional thinking about that moment. The gift was a basketball t-shirt of the Syracuse Orange (Orangemen back then) and it said "Beast of the East" on it. I can still picture it and where I was in that moment. I saw it and then cried my eyes out for what seemed like hours. It wasn't so much because of the gift or missing the team and the game I loved, but because of how it felt to know someone else cared. I was old enough to understand that someone else thought enough about me to not only get me a gift but find out where I lived and bring it to me to make sure I received it. It was the best present I got that year, by far. The one that meant the most.

I never knew if Mr. J knew what was going on with me at home. I never knew if *anyone* really knew. But there's a part of me that thinks many knew more than I ever thought they did, because of little things that always seemed to happen like this. Ultimately, I think God made sure I always had some guardian angels around me. Mr. Jamieson was one of those people. My other basketball coach, Mr. Patrick Campany was too. God made sure I was surrounded my good people. Angels, so to speak. There were some days when, even as a young kid, I didn't want to continue living the life I was living. Suicide was always right there lingering in the background for me, even as a child. It was school and things like this—people like this— who kept me going. The things that kept me surviving. The things that kept me moving forward. The things that gave me *hope*.

Even with those people around me at school and having a small bit of hope, it still wasn't easy and led me to even run away once. I didn't realize just how significant that was until I was an adult and understood what could've happened to me that night.

It was the middle of the night and I had it planned for weeks. I remember the dog across the street always being outside and always barking anytime anyone was around. My plan was to get on my bike and take the back way around and out of our trailer park, so as not to disturb the dog, get him barking, and be discovered. And that's exactly what I did. My plan was to make it to my Aunt Sally's house, as she was such an amazing mother figure to me when I was able to see her. I was so happy when my parents would go on trips and Sal would take me in. So, my goal was to get to her that night, but I didn't make it.

I rode my bike for what ended up being 30 miles, from Watertown to Mannsville, in the middle of the night. It was dark and cold. I don't think I realize how dangerous it really was. At one point, I had a dog chasing me. Sometime later, I had a man stop alongside me in a car and ask me if I wanted a ride. Many times, I was in the middle of nowhere with no street lights. And at one point, I was even riding my bike on the highway.

THE SHELF

Crazy.

Ultimately, while stuck in the dark in the middle of a cornfield somewhere, I doubled back to the town of Adams and ended up knocking on the door of my English teacher, Mr. Leon Caster. He welcomed me in with open arms, gave me a place to sleep and called my father to let him know I was safe. I don't remember exactly what I told Mr. Caster that night, or how I even know where he lived, but that's where I ended up. God's plan I'm sure. His hands were all over me that night to keep me safe, I'm sure.

My father came to get me the next morning. He wasn't happy. Once I got home, we all sat in the living room to discuss my punishment for running away. There was no talk about why I chose to run away. There was no desire to resolve any issues. There were no questions asked of me. All they cared about was the fact that I got the school involved by going to a teacher's house and how they were going to punish me for doing it. So, two more weeks confined to my room starting at the ceiling doing nothing. No big deal—I was already used to it.

It's really no wonder no one ever really saw me outside of school and may not have known what was going on with me at home.

I rarely went to dances or proms or many school events that happened outside of normal school hours. One of the only dances I ever remember going to was on the last day of school in eighth grade. It was in the gym, and everyone was excited about the summer and our becoming freshmen and starting on a new journey in high school. This dance has always stayed etched in my memory, even thirty years later, as that's when I felt just a glimpse of what I thought love was for the first time. And ultimately, it would end up being when I felt how much those sorts of feelings hurt for the first time.

Her name was Maria; she was beautiful, smart, and funny. In those days, I wasn't shy in school; and despite what I had been through, I was confident in some things. I had no problem asking Maria to dance that day. I wasn't sure she'd say yes, but I asked anyway. She obliged, and the four minutes we danced together was like fireworks for me. The way we touched and the closeness I felt was indescribable. The butterflies, the racing hearts—there weren't any words to be spoken; there wasn't a need for any. It was a first for me. The world seemed to completely go away for a while, and that was something I so desperately needed.

It was the last dance; it was the last day of school. What I felt was the beginning of something magical. Maria walked away that day, and I just knew that she had to have felt something too. I was so ready to spend the summer with her, talking to her, and seeing where life would take us.

The summer came and went, and I didn't hear from her. Life back then wasn't like it is today with texting and social media. I never lost hope though as I was excited about my feelings and knew she had to have had them too. We didn't have cell phones, Facebook, and the Internet back then, so not hearing from her all summer didn't necessarily produce giant red flags of "I'm not interested" to me. I just knew in my heart that when I'd see her again at school, the spark would still be there just like it was in that dance, and we would pick right up where we left off.

As the last days of summer came and went, I grew more excited about seeing her and starting something great. I thought about her every day. I remember thinking about how envious I was of all the other "couples" I always saw walking the halls holding hands before class, and I envisioned that often for Maria and me when school began. This was my time; she was the one. Finally, some good in my life to look forward to.

Unfortunately, it didn't happen as I had hoped, and it was awful for me. I spent an entire summer on this amazing high; this euphoria of feelings I had never felt before was amazing. It was the very first time I felt those types of feelings. But when school started, and I saw her for the very first time, it was almost as if Maria didn't even know me. It was like our moment had never happened. And in her world, as I stood there about to start this school year I had so looked forward to, I just didn't exist. I was crushed.

My self-esteem almost hit rock bottom after that. It was hard enough at home to literally be beaten down physically; it was hard enough to be told at home that I was worthless and made to feel that I'd never be good enough for anyone or anything. Now this.

THE SHELF

This hurt in different ways because of how safe school had always been for me. It was a defining moment in my life, as far as relationships go. Expectations I had for myself weren't all that high after that. I was nothing but a skinny little nerd with cheap clothes and funny glasses. Friends I used to have suddenly weren't friends anymore in high school. I felt worthless and completely alone. I was starting to believe all the horrible things I was being told about who I was and where I'd end up.

My thoughts turned negative, and my self-worth was completely gone. Why did I think Maria would ever want someone like me anyway? I never existed in her world; it was just some fantasy I had built up in my own mind. I made that moment we had something that it never was. These were the things I told myself after I looked at her, and she just looked right through me. Suddenly, my safe place didn't feel so safe; and Maria was just another person who, like everyone else, didn't want me.

It was very confusing time for me then. I had already been through a lot, but the personal part of my life with girls was relatively new. Regardless, I moved on and got over it, and school remained my safe place. After that, and as I got older, I really started to listen intently to all the kids around me. Everyone talked so positively about their lives, their families, and looking forward to the weekends, holidays, and summer vacations. I always remember being so confused about that early on because it was nothing like my life and the way things were. In fact, it was the opposite for me. I found peace at school and with my teachers and friends, not at home. And I remember daydreaming often about just finding that same peace they talked about somewhere else in my world—peace in a place where I wouldn't be discarded and feel alone all the time, a place where I would feel completely safe and know I was loved unconditionally.

> The LORD tests the righteous, but his soul hates
> the wicked and the one who loves violence.
>
> —Psalm 11:5

CHAPTER 5

My Solace

I talked earlier about the significance that basketball had in my life. It was the only thing I could do that would kind of make the world go away for me for a while and allow me to just feel free. While my first experience with that was at a real young age when I could barely get the ball to the rim and wasn't old enough to comprehend much, my real experiences with basketball and peace came later during junior high school and high school with my grandparents.

Frank and Fern Trowbridge; they were my mother's parents who had been together for more than seventy years. They were true examples of what true love and family was about. Once I left my mother to live with my father, you'd probably think that my relationship with her parents would suffer. It didn't. In fact, the relationship with them only strengthened throughout my teen years as I spent most of my weekends and summers at their house when my parents would allow it.

Staying with my grandparents on the farm would normally be a weekend thing. It worked like clockwork most of the time. Friday mornings I would pack my bag and lug it onto the bus in the morning to take to school. I'd go to my locker in the band room (I was a trumpet player) and stuff the bag in there because it was always too large to fit in my normal book locker—and because band was my last class of the day for most years that I can remember. The parking lot was also right outside the band room doors, and that's where my Gram would always be waiting to pick me up.

THE SHELF

Gram would always greet me with a hug and kiss and ask me how my day was. She was an insurance agent, and her office was downtown in the town the school was in. Because her work day wasn't over yet when school let out for the day, we'd always go back to her office where I'd just hang out until she was done working at five o'clock. Her office was downtown and located right next to a little store where I would go to buy candy and other things my parents never let me have. (My father had a purple Crown Royal bag full of quarters in his desk drawer, and I'd often take some out before school on those Fridays so I'd have some money to spend there.) The little things with them made me happy.

Once Gram was done with work, she would always have to work to track me down, then we'd go to the grocery store to get food for the weekend. My favorite aisle was the cereal aisle where she'd always let me pick out the cereal I wanted—generally the kind that had the best prize inside. I was never allowed to eat anything but plain cornflakes with no sugar growing up with my stepmother, so this was always a special treat that I very much looked forward to. (I tried putting sugar on my cornflakes from time to time at home. You already read about how that turned out for me.) Gram and I walked through the store, got my cereal, and then ended in the frozen section where we'd get ice cream for the weekend too. She would always get French vanilla for Gramp; it was cookies and cream for me. After that, we'd head home to see Gramp.

Gramp was an amazing man. A funny man, an old Navy torpedoman on submarines during World War II, Frank was the only true father figure I ever had. He taught me about responsibility and hard work; he taught me about respect and treating women right; he showed me what hard work looked like as he always worked so hard in the garden, mowing the grass on the acres of land the farm was on, painting fences on the property, and doing anything you can imagine would need to be done on a farm that didn't have cattle or crops. Other than my cousin John, who also spent a lot of time there with them, Gramp was the only real male role model I ever had to look up to. He was the only true example of a father I ever had. I grew up spending so much time with him, learning the value of a dollar, the meaning of hard work, and what it meant to be a real father, husband, and friend. Above all else, he made me feel loved. He wasn't always one to hug you and kiss you and tell you he loved you, but his actions showed it. Looking back now, I know that more than ever. It's evident in how I treat my own children today. If ever I've been a good father to my own children, it's because of Gramp, the great example he set, and the many values he instilled in me.

He was hilarious. His ability to fart on command was well-known amongst us grandkids in the family. I'll never forget his "pull my finger" jokes and how he'd yell my name, let one go, then immediately start running as if his flatulence was jet-propelling his sudden running speed at seventy years old when he'd start running around the room. He was amazing and like that every day; he was genuinely one of a kind.

Gram was a loving, caring soul. She had a huge heart and loved unlike anyone I'd ever met. I think she knew how hard childhood was for me and did everything she could to rescue me from it. As a child, she wasn't going to discuss with me all the things she knew about my father, but I know she knew about them. As I got older and stayed with them, I started to realize how much she knew. I once found a newspaper clipping in Gram's home office about my father being charged with rape. I took it to Gram and asked her about it, and she quickly took it and didn't discuss it any further with me. I still don't know what that was all about. But honestly, I wasn't surprised; after all, I had seen him do some horrible things with my very own eyes and was still carrying those haunting visions around with me at the time. But Gram was not going to add to those burdens. She took the clipping from me, changed the subject, and took me away from it. It was symbolic of what I think she always tried to do for me: take me away from the bad stuff and show me as much love as she could in the time we had together.

THE SHELF

The thing I remember most about the farm was the great number of hours I spent on the basketball goal that Gramp had put up on a telephone pole in the yard next to the house. I attribute my world-famous ninja basketball skills to all the hours spent there shooting on that goal to get away from the world for a while. (Okay, I may have exaggerated a little there.)

I remember thinking about so much, wondering why my life was the way it was and why things had been the way they were. Why didn't my mother want me? Why did my father do what he did? Why didn't Maria like me? What was going to happen to me in my life? How was I going to turn out? I had *very* adult conversations with myself about my life, my future, and what I was going to do with it all. I never spoke of it or had these types of conversations with anyone else. These were answers I had to find on my own. These were things I had to figure out on my own. As a teenager, the struggle was so real, the burden was so large, and I had already been through so much.

Sunday nights were always filled with ice cream, Gram scratching my back, me combing Gramp's one strand of hair over on his bald head, and the three of us watching *Barbara Mandrell and the Mandrell Sisters* and *The Golden Girls* on television in the den. Nights like these are likely why I still have such an affinity for all *The Golden Girls* reruns still playing on television today. Don't judge me.

DAVID K. DEREMER

I have so many amazing memories of my time on the farm with my grandparents, far too many to mention. Gram would take me to church on Sundays where my spiritual journey started. I still remember singing "Jesus and Me" with my mom at that same church when I was really little. I used to get blank cassette tapes and record Casey Kasem's *American Top 40* every Sunday, so I always had the best and most current music in my Walkman—a Walkman that Gram bought for me. Gramp would purposely turn country music up really loud to wake me up on Monday mornings. I would bang on the piano in the formal living room and drive Gram nuts. I'd work in the garden with Gramp. So many memories, so much love.

Together, they were the American Dream. They had a love that was undeniable and were two people who lived and loved with everything they had. Gramp built their home with his own two hands; and thankfully, my own kids were able to see them and visit the only real solace I ever had in my life. The farm was solace for many, more so because of the two who lived in it than the farm itself.

THE SHELF

I wish I had more time with them in my adult years. It's hard some days to know that they're both gone. You always have regret about time you've missed, especially when you make plans to visit that never pan out. My military career away from home didn't help that much. It seems we are always too busy for the important things until we realize those things are gone. Again, I wish I could've had more time. I love them both and know they're both safe and smiling and happy for me now.

If I could say anything to them now, I'd just thank them for loving me and being my rock, my ear, and my shoulder to cry on for so long when no one else was. I'd say thank you for being rare, one-of-a-kind examples of how people should be and how they should live. I'd tell them that I love them more than they'll ever know, and that most everything I am and everything that's good in my life now is because of the man they both made me. I ask God every day to take care of them. Heaven became an even better place the minute they both arrived there.

So now faith, hope, and love abide, these
three; but the greatest of these is love.

—1 Corinthians 13:13

CHAPTER 6

The Reunion

In the middle of my junior year, things changed. The abuse and hard times continued at home, and my self-esteem was at an all-time low. I had gotten used to living this sort of life, but I was getting older and getting more and more tired of being beaten on, being told I would never amount to anything in life, and made to feel like I was worthless by my stepmother. All this while my father would sit there and do absolutely nothing about it.

There came a point in time when I finally stepped up and challenged my stepmother, not physically, but verbally. (I was never a big kid as I tipped the scales at just above 140 pounds as a seventeen-year-old.) I remember getting punched and kicked in the kitchen one day and making a comment about calling the child abuse hotline on her if she ever hit me again. Of course, that prompted her to follow me down the hallway, grab me by the hair, and yank me around while beating me more. Once she was done, I went to my room and just sat there feeling helpless and trapped, just as I always did. Shortly after my father returned home, she apparently told him what I had said. I remember sitting at my desk in my room and seeing him step into my doorway. It was there that he threatened me, saying that if I ever did that or said anything like that to my stepmother again, it would be a very bad day for me.

It was a surprise for my father to get involved at all, really. He worked, came home, and did nothing but sit in his chair watching television or playing his video games. It was almost as if he was completely oblivious to what was going on in our home, but I knew he knew; He just didn't care. He was very selfish. I cared so little for him and had so little respect for him as a father at this point anyway, so his being absent didn't matter to me much; in fact, it was welcomed. But in this moment when he said that to me, it was the first time he ever even acknowledged the abuse in our home, whether he viewed it as such or not.

I sat there thinking he should've been on my side. Again, I didn't expect anything different, already knowing the type of person he truly was, but he should have been on my side. He didn't care about anyone but himself. He never cared about his kids. He had a daughter before he met my mother whom he never saw or talked to; he never talked to or saw my brother anymore at this point; and here I was living with him, and it was very clear that he didn't really care about me either. I wasn't surprised at his response but wasn't going to take the threat lying down either. As I said before, I was a smart kid despite the things they both put me through growing up.

A month or so prior, I had reconnected with my mother after many years of not seeing her. I had spent so much time with my grandparents on the weekends while I was in high school that I had the opportunity to talk to her more on the phone and see her a few times as the years went by. My grandparents did the best they could to try and reunite us again, I think. Gram and Gramp knew the situation I was in, but I don't think they could do much about it—no one really could. So they did the best they could to give me all the things I was missing, to include having some sort of relationship with their daughter, my mother.

I don't remember the specific details of it all now, but I do remember that my mother came to pick me up a couple times at my dad's house to go to the movies or the mall with her and my brother and stepsister Charlotte. At this point, I'm not sure what my stepfather thought or knew about my situation, but I do remember that I never went to spend much time with them at their house. My mother just came to get me, and we went places to spend time together. It was at this point that I think she started to realize how dire my situation really was. My brother had already stopped visiting me and my father because he too was getting beaten when he'd come on the weekends; and now with my mother and I talking, she was starting to hear more and more. It's hard for me to say why no one tried to get me out of there before then. I guess I'll never know. Maybe there just wasn't enough to prove the abuse; and honestly, it happened so frequently, I guess I just thought it was normal all those years. I never really said much to anyone until then. And maybe that's why things happened the way they did when they did.

After spending a couple weekends with my mother, I was starting to feel love like I hadn't felt before. I was happy when I thought of being with her and my brother again, and our short times together always seemed like they were just that—short. It didn't really hit me as to how good I felt with them until I would return home and get just the opposite. And more times than not, I'd be met with sarcastic "oh, so did you have a good time with your mother?" comments and questions. Of course, being the smart-mouthed teenager I had become after enduring so much, I would often reply with "yup, I sure did" and then proceed to either get my butt beat again or get a tongue-lashing like you wouldn't believe. It was the norm; I was used to it.

It all started to change the day I wrote "the note." Now, you must understand my stepmother. Not only was she the type of person like I've already described, she was also the type of person who would go through my room every day, turning everything upside down looking for things I might be hiding. I was never allowed to have sweets or anything like that, so sometimes when we had basketball games, I'd sneak to the store next to our school and buy candy and cakes and other stuff with the money my grandfather gave me for working with him doing chores during the weekends I spent there. No matter where my "stash" was hidden, my stepmother would always find it. She was always looking for a reason to beat me or give me a hard time. And this happened every single day.

Of course, at this point, I was clever enough to use this to my advantage. Again, I wasn't a dumb kid. I wrote a very long note to myself, and in that note contained the very specific details of how I felt about my life, my stepmother, being beaten and berated daily, having no friends, never being allowed to leave the house, and everything else I had endured for so long. I poured my heart out onto the paper, just as I've always been able to do. I left no stone unturned as to how I felt about everything, what I wanted out of life, and where I wanted to be. After spending so much time with my grandparents, my mother, and my brother in those weeks prior and feeling love that I hadn't felt in years, I knew that I wanted to be with them—and that was exactly what I wanted my stepmother to see. And if I had to endure a beating after her seeing it, it was a risk worth taking if the result was even close to what I had hoped it'd end up being.

I had a small Timex clock on the top left corner of my desk. Of course, it was the eighties, so it was nothing more than just a regular square white clock with a real face on it. I'm not sure much of anything was digital back then. But it was just the right size to "hide" a square folded-up sheet of paper (ya know, like my note). And when placed just right under the clock (of course, there had to be just a little of it sticking out to guarantee its discovery), it fit perfectly. So that's where I put it that night when I finished writing it. Then I went to sleep, woke up and went to school, and waited.

I came home from school the next day and just as I suspected, the note was gone (it's almost as if I had planned it). Nothing was said to me until my father got home, and that's when all hell broke loose. He stood in the doorway as I sat at my desk doing homework, just as he had the day he threatened me after I made the "child abuse hotline" comment. He went on a tirade about how my mother never wanted me, and it was clear he was just trying to hurt me with all the words coming out of his mouth. He wasn't aware of how numb I was to all the verbal abuse already, apparently. He went on and on about it all and what I had written in the note about going to live with my mother. Ultimately, he said that if that's what I wanted, he'd go ahead and call her and tell her to come get me.

Immediately, I had flashbacks of that day when I heard almost those exact same words from my stepfather and my own mother allowing it to happen. Now, my father was about to kick me to the curb as a sixteen-year-old; only this time, it's exactly what I wanted. So he called my mother.

I don't remember specifics, but I do remember crying and talking to her on the phone and her asking me if that's what I wanted. I told her it was, and that's when she told me she wanted me there, and that she had talked to Michael already, and that he wanted me there too. Here it was, more than ten years later, and things were about to flip 180 degrees completely. The stepfather who told me to go live with my father and the mother who let it happen were now rescuing me from the situation I was in. They wanted me, and they were coming to save me.

For ten years while living with my father and stepmother, I had attended the same school. Everything I knew was there, including all my friends and that support system of teachers I talked about in previous chapters. I loved South Jefferson Central School, and being a Spartan was something I was always proud of. I wasn't sure what was going to happen or when with my mother at the time of my dad's comments, but nothing happened that night. I went to bed as I normally did and went to school the next day without knowing what would happen next.

I was in biology class when it was time to go. My mother was in the office waiting for me. I'll never forget getting the message as I sat next to my good friend Anne and knew I was leaving her. She was always the one constant in my life all the way through school. The one who always was there for me, no matter what. I remember her looking confused as I got up to leave, and all I could do was say goodbye with tears in my eyes. I was so in love with her in school, although the feelings were never reciprocated. We were such great friends, though, and she was always there for me when I needed her even though I never spoke much to her about what I was dealing with at home. I think she must have had some idea, though. Regardless, in this moment, all I knew was that this was probably going to be goodbye. And it was.

I walked out of the classroom, out of the school, and out of that life I knew. From elementary school and the principal, Mr. Kane; teachers Ms. Haight and Mrs. Cooper; all my coaches, Coach LaDuke, Coach Jamieson, Coach Company; my band teachers and

THE SHELF

mentors, Mrs. Greene, Mrs. Badour, Mr. LaClair, Mr. Rudari; to my friends Anne, Andy, Tammie, Jen, and Tommy—I missed them all every single day during those last two years of high school spent at Thousand Islands High School. For most of my young life, South Jefferson and all those people I mentioned were my saviors and my getaway from a world at home I didn't want to be in. They were the ones who cared; they were the ones who looked out for me; they were the ones who were important to me; they gave me peace at a time when I could have chosen to end my life and finally stop all the pain I was feeling; they saved me.

Despite walking out that day and missing them, I knew there were going to be better days ahead; I was confident in that. I was headed to a place where things would be better; I was headed to a place where things would be stable; I was headed to a place where things would be safe.

> And when he had said these things, he knelt down and prayed with them all. And there was much weeping on the part of all; they embraced Paul and kissed him, being sorrowful most of all because of the word he had spoken, that they would not see his face again. And they accompanied him to the ship.
>
> —Acts 20:36–38

CHAPTER 7

The Next Phase

First, let me make something very clear. As I sit here now as someone who I feel is a changed man and a Christian man, don't think for one second that I have always been proud of who I've been in my adult life. The impact my childhood had on my future was extremely significant. And while I refuse to relinquish total responsibility, point fingers, or not be accountable for many of my own actions, the things that happened to me early on in my life did have an effect.

I was a cheater; I was a liar; I was arguably the most arrogant man on the planet, as some of my longtime friends (if there are even any left) would likely attest. I cared about nothing but myself for a very long time and didn't care about the people I hurt along the way.

In my younger adult days, I considered myself a charming, athletic good-looking man, and I never had any problem getting attention. Once I joined the air force and started really coming into my own, the attention became even more frequent, and I loved every second of it—all of it. It was quite the drastic change compared to my younger days where the clothes I wore, the glasses on my face, and my 120 pounds screamed nothing but "nerd" to everyone around me. I couldn't turn a head during high school if I wanted to. So when you grow up being a nerd and are constantly demeaned by your parents and suddenly people start paying attention to you, it can change you. And for me, it changed me for the worse.

My arrogance after joining the air force was out of control. It turned me into someone I would end up despising. It took me the better part of twenty years to finally figure that part of me out, the part that was shaped by a childhood with no self-esteem. But at least I was able to figure it out. Counseling works wonders; faith in God works wonders. My arrogance was a coping mechanism for the childhood trauma brewing inside of me that I didn't even realize was there yet. Again, I was able to figure it all out finally, but not before it cost me just about everything that was important to me in most of my adult life. My marriage, friends, and maybe much more than I even know about as I sit here in this moment.

Looking back now after much counseling, I know being that guy was my way to cope with a lifetime of being put on the shelf. A lifetime of being cast aside, ridiculed, and told I would never amount to anything. After joining the air force, I got attention, then I wanted attention, and then I ultimately just craved attention. I wanted to be that centerpiece after a childhood of being put on a shelf I never knew existed, and I was becoming it. I wanted the attention from whoever would give it; and in some cases, from people I should have never gotten it from. And all while I was married to a woman who, early in our marriage, had always put me first and loved me unconditionally while I always put her on the shelf. Yes, that's right; I put her on the shelf. It was something she never deserved, just as it's something I never deserved. We will get into that more later in this book.

My last year and a half of high school was great with my mother and stepfather. We had the normal ups and downs, but I finally had stability, positivity, and structure. My stepfather was strict but fair and always tried to instill traits in us that would set us up for success as adults. From conserving water and things on a tight budget to helping us get jobs to earn money and understand the value of a dollar, he was what a father was supposed to be. Firm but fair, that was Michael.

Because of my stable and positive home, I became a scholar-athlete in those last two years of high school and an elite musician. I had played the trumpet for seven years prior to that but had become a standout at Thousand Islands. Then I would become the top trumpet player in New York State my junior and senior years of high school, having the highest performance solo scores at the highest solo difficulty level in state competition. Because of that, I was first chair, first trumpet in the area all-state and bicounty bands. I was selected to the state stage band. My grades soared, and I had practically become fluent in French from years of taking it in school and making it to the highest level French class that New York state offered. Everything seemed to be falling into place.

As graduation time neared, I sent applications to colleges but really didn't have any intentions of getting accepted. For years, I wanted to join the air force and always had "Aim High" posters on my walls next to posters and Sports Illustrated cut out photos of Michael Jordan, Larry Bird, and Magic Johnson, and twenty-by-thirty-inch replicas of Celtics championship banners I made myself and hung from my ceiling.

People often ask me why I joined the air force, and I really have no idea. My cousin John was a couple of years older than me and had joined the Marines, and he was always someone I looked up to. I'm not sure that was the reason for my choice, but as I look back on it now, all I can say is that it was probably the easiest option for me to get away. The easiest way to leave the horrible situation I was in. There was no way my father and stepmother were going to pay for college as they always told me that once I graduated from high school, they were putting me out on my own. Maybe I felt as a child that the military was my only option. I really don't know why that was always my dream. It was just what I wanted to do. God's plan for me, I suppose.

I met a girl named Darci when I first arrived at Thousand Islands High School, and we began dating. It was my first real experience in a relationship, and the euphoria of it all was amazing for me at the time. We had our ups and downs, which would be significant, but it was nice to have that opportunity to be with someone on a different level than I ever had before. I was coming into my own as a man and started to feel certain ways about certain things.

I struggled with personal relationships, and I'd find out why that was many years later. Not to say that my unknown struggle with PTSD was the sole cause of my breakups back then; but looking back, I know it had to have played a part, especially early on when I had no idea of the internal chaos going on in my head that was impacting every decision I would make in every relationship I would ever have.

At first with Darci, I wanted her; but then when I had her or she showed interest, I didn't want her anymore. It was a vicious cycle and one I'm not proud of today. You'll learn more later about why that's significant. But we made it for quite a while; we had so many great times together when times were good. I lost my virginity to her the summer before our senior year; and with that being the case, it truly seemed like this was a relationship that was going to last for a very long time.

I ended up living with her and her parents for a while, after a blowup at home with my mother. She kicked me out of the house, and I had nowhere else to go. Again, I felt as if my mother didn't want me, so I called Darci and told her what was going on and asked if I could stay with her. Her parents said it was okay. What was only supposed to end up being a night or two ended up being the entire summer and until February of 1993 when I left for the air force. Her parents were amazing to me, always supported me, and had a genuine and sincere interest in me. I will always be thankful for them and the time I was able to spend with them.

Darci would end up going off to college in the fall, and I still stayed with her parents. She would come home to visit when she could. It wasn't easy for me. On top of that, I had to deal with some issues I had with one of her previous boyfriends trying to get back with her. I could never fully get past them. I guess you could say that these were my first real trust issues. He had shown an interest in her again while we were together, and that crushed me even though she said nothing happened with them, and I had nothing to worry about. This was the first time that I started to feel insecurities, doubt, and fear about being abandoned again in a real relationship. The separation bothered me. I just didn't feel good; I didn't feel right. I was lost and couldn't find my way.

After a year or so of dating, I asked Darci to marry me on Christmas Day in 1992. A short time before that, arguments and insecurities caused a huge problem for us, and I ended up showing her the ring during one of our fights. So she knew a proposal was coming. She said "yes," likely because of my leaving for the air force in February and because of her own feelings that she'd lose me, much like the ones I had when she left for school. It was an engagement destined for failure as I don't think it was based on anything other than fear. Sure, we both thought we loved each other, but it was the fear of separation that prompted the engagement. We tried to make it through basic training, technical schools, and everything else. We tried.

I ended up getting stationed at Patrick Air Force Base in Cocoa Beach, Florida, and I remember Darci making plans to move there when she graduated. Initially, I was excited; but after a little time went by, that just wasn't in the cards for me. During tech school where I learned my air force job, I had heard rumors of Darci's cheating on me, and that didn't settle well with me. It was abandonment on a different level. I never found out if the rumors were true, but I don't think it would've mattered. Not with what I know about myself now. But after nights of tears and worrying about the rumors, I decided I wouldn't worry about it and try to make it work.

Once I got to Florida though, things changed, and you'll read more about that later too. I came into my own, started getting attention as I've mentioned, and that changed my life. While still engaged to Darci, I was exploring a brand-new world I never knew existed. Women were interested in me; women thought I was attractive. After a lifetime of feeling inadequate, worthless, and unworthy, I was slowly becoming the center of attention. I had an amazing time during that first year stationed in Florida, living a life I never knew was possible.

Unfortunately, Darci fell victim to the new me that was emerging, and I ended the relationship a little while after getting stationed there in September of 1993. After arriving in Florida, I was enjoying the single life. I was happy. The air force was going to be awesome.

CHAPTER 8

My Career, Part 1

As I touched on a little earlier, it's really hard to put my finger on why I chose the military as a career. Looking back, I could say that it was because of family influences as my grandfather, stepfather, and cousins had all been in the military. Of course, I didn't truly grasp what they had done in the military back then, nor did we talk about it, but I imagine it was just in my blood and meant to happen for me to join too. Or maybe I felt it was the only choice I had to get away from a childhood I was always trying to escape from.

My first memories of wanting to join the air force specifically are when I was in junior high school. I remember seeing air force brochures at school and also some photos of air force jets with the "Aim High, Air Force" motto and old air force logo on them. I ended up bringing some home and putting them up on the walls in my room, and from there, my initial thoughts of joining the air force had begun. Again, I really don't have a reason why these thoughts started in the first place or how I ever thought they'd become my reality. Over the years, so many people have asked me why I joined the air force, and I've never really known a good reason why. Strange, I know, but God has a funny way of making things happen just as He wants them too. Things that will ultimately lead you down the path you're truly meant for whether you can see it ahead of time or not.

I remember flying over the lights of San Antonio, Texas, that night on February 11th, 1993. I had never been on an airplane before, nor had I really left the state of New York in my eighteen years. I had been to Pennsylvania to visit my grandmother each year; but other than that, I had never been anywhere like this. So the entire experience was interesting. In addition to that, unlike many others, I didn't have any preparation for basic training and hadn't been told what to expect when I got there. I was a naive young, eighteen-year-old kid who had finally escaped the life I once knew to start over new in a place, doing something I knew absolutely nothing about.

I don't remember being nervous or apprehensive about basic training. As the plane started its descent into San Antonio, the lights got bigger and brighter, and I was ready to see just what was in store for me. I missed Darci at the time, and that part was hard, but I was definitely ready to start my new life as an adult and experience all the amazing things that life had to offer that I never grew up knowing. Of course, that lack of nerves and apprehension changed the second I walked into the terminal and started being ushered around by larger-than-life military people carrying around big black hats. Suddenly, this air force thing just got real.

Despite my inexperience and lack of preparation for basic training, I was very successful during those six weeks. I've always considered myself to be a natural leader, and our basic training instructors apparently saw some of that in me too. Sometimes, though not exclusively, Basic Military Training instructors will choose the older members of the flight for certain leadership positions. Generally, these elder trainees have some leadership qualities from previous civilian employment, are generally more mature, and are able to handle responsibility better than others under stress. But choosing older trainees is not a hard and fast rule. Our training instructors, or TIs, have full authority to select their flight's leaders using whatever criteria they wish. It's not unusual for some of the initial choices to not work out, and instructors may make changes to the flight leadership after a short observation period.

The dorm chief is the top leader of all the trainees in the flight. This trainee is responsible for making sure that all orders, operations, and instructor instructions are carried out correctly when the instructors aren't around. A trainee doesn't make many friends if they're selected as dorm chief, but they certainly were taught how to be an effective leader while being taught to be an air force airman.

To assist the dorm chief in this great responsibility, the flight gets split into four elements, and an element leader is chosen to be in charge of each. This was the role I was chosen to fill during my time in basic training. My job was to report any issues to the dorm chief and assist in assuring that members of my element complied with all orders and instructions. Some of these included being on time for appointments, shaving, having beds made, keeping lockers clean, and many other necessary things.

The bad news about being a dorm chief or an element leader meant that in addition to being responsible for things I did wrong myself, I had the added pleasure of being responsible for the many things that so many members of my element did wrong as well. It was my first taste of what leadership was and the place where many of my own personal leadership philosophies and approaches were born. I'll be forever thankful for having the opportunity to lead early and understand early why having real leadership skills in this military was important. Not only did I have to demonstrate to our leaders that I was capable, I also had to show my subordinates that despite my position, we were all part of a team.

I carried all those leadership traits with me throughout my career and continued to shape and hone those skills every single year until I retired. I knew I would never be too old and never have too much rank to stop learning how to lead.

Basic training was great, and I learned a lot. However, what I learned the most was that you can't necessarily believe your recruiter when he tells you before you sign enlistment papers that you have the guaranteed job that you want. I'll never forget the day I realized I didn't.

We were in line outside of the administrative building waiting to go in and see what jobs we'd have after basic training. We'd also get an idea where we'd be going for school upon the completion of basic training. I can still picture it as the instructors were yelling at everyone and telling people to get into one of two lines—the "open general" line for those who didn't have a guaranteed job and the "guaranteed job" line for those who did. We all had paperwork that apparently told us one way or the other; but of course, I had no clue. All I knew was that I had a guaranteed job in the public affairs career field, and that "guaranteed job" line was where I was going. Even the graduation article about me in our local newspaper back home said I had a guaranteed job in the public affairs field. I had no reason to think I didn't, based on all I knew and what the recruiter had told me.

Of course, I got further in line. One of the instructors checked my paperwork, and then almost made my ears bleed as he screamed at me with a decibel level I don't think I had ever heard from a human being before. Let's see…I was in the wrong line, couldn't follow instructions, and apparently had all sorts of mental problems according to the training instructor who had a hold of me. I can only laugh about it now; but at the time, not only was I being screamed at with this dude's hat bouncing off my face for being in the wrong place, now I had no idea what job I would have or what my air force future was going to consist of.

It could have been worse. I could have been a cop or a cook. However, when the time finally came, there was one choice on my list that seemed okay: communications computer systems operator.

After I graduated from basic training, I left for Keesler Air Force Base in Mississippi for communications computer systems school. I had no idea what it was about or what it would be like, but Mississippi wasn't too far from Texas, and I figured I'd just take it all in stride and do the best I could with the situation I was in. I got there, got settled in, learned the rules of the dorm and all that was involved, and eventually started school. It wasn't long after that that I'd soon realize I was in way over my head in more ways than one, and the path ahead that God had already paved for me with regard to my military career really started to take shape.

I wish I could say that my failures at school were because I just didn't understand the job and what I was doing, but if I'm being honest with myself and with you, I have to admit that there was more to it than just that. While I did severely struggle with the curriculum and testing, I was also involved with a woman at school who had more of my attention than my books did.

Her name was Katy, and she was much older than I was at the time. She was the most beautiful woman I had ever seen in my life, and I immediately fell in love with her. I loved who she was and how she was with me. She was the type of woman who just stops you dead in your tracks—beautiful big blue eyes and a smile that made my heart melt in a second. Of course, I was engaged to Darci at the time, so feeling like I was feeling real love with Katy was confusing, especially when they were feelings that I never felt with the woman I was engaged to at the time. I was still so young, and my experience with relationships was still in its infancy. I was with Darci, the only woman I had ever really dated seriously, but the feelings I had for Katy were undeniable—and feelings I just couldn't overlook or give up on. It was the first time I had ever felt those sorts of feelings in my life.

Katy graduated from school and left Keesler about a month after we had met. We spent as much time together as we could, although I could sense that she wasn't in the same place as I was about our relationship. I was supposed to meet her at the base exchange to say goodbye the day that she left. I was there, but she never showed. I waited as long as I could but had to get back to our squadron for formation. I got back and into position, and as I stood in line, one of my friends who was a red rope (the student leader of our squadron, much like the dorm chief in basic training) came up to me, handed me a note, and told me that Katy wanted him to tell me goodbye. She had seen him earlier in the day, talked to him, and gave him the note. I was crushed and can still remember it and the feelings I had in that moment so vividly. Suddenly, this woman whom I felt these extraordinary feelings for had walked out of my life, and I would never see her again.

After that, things got increasingly difficult for me. I was lost about Katy and feeling abandoned once again and would often find myself daydreaming about my feelings for her and the reasons why I had them. I went to school every day after that; but honestly, I was never truly there. My mind was elsewhere after that, and that would end up being a serious problem for me as I continued to struggle and ultimately failed out of the course.

I wasn't sure what was going to happen after that. I was a believer in God back then, but my faith definitely wasn't what it is today.

And I didn't often think *God has a better plan for me* when adversity would strike in my life back then. I wasn't sure of the process or what would happen next; all I knew was that I had exceeded the amount of chances I would get and now had a meeting with the squadron commander to talk about it all. *My future in the air force could be over before it even starts,* I thought to myself.

I don't remember many of the specifics of that meeting, but I can still picture where I was seated and remember being very nervous. The commander talked to me about the importance of finding the right people for the right jobs and asked me what it was that I wanted. I told him I wanted to be in the air force, and that it was all I had ever wanted for as long as I could remember. Beyond that, I'm not sure what convinced him to give me another chance, but he did.

I found myself in the personnel office later that day, where I was put into what they called a "pipeline." I was able to choose five jobs from a list of jobs, and while there were no guarantees that I'd get one of those five, they'd consider my choices when deciding what to do with me next. The pipeline was set up to simply spit out a name from a list of applicants (likely others who had failed out of jobs just like me) and an available job opening (likely ones that no one wanted) and match those things together. That's how they decided what to do with this particular group of people. So as you can imagine, I wasn't confident I'd get any of the jobs I had chosen. I'm sure the process was a bit more complex and more involved than just spitting out names and jobs, but that's how it was explained to me at the time. And because of that, I had pretty much accepted the fact that I'd probably be a cop or a cook, and I'd have to just be happy with what I got. In my heart, I knew this was the bed I had made for myself, and now I just had to lie in it.

When the personnel specialist finally got back to me, I was given my very first job. I was hoping I'd get an admin job so I could just stay at Keesler for that school, get it over with, and then go home on leave. But no, that wasn't God's plan for me. In fact, it couldn't have been further from what I had planned and what I wanted.

I looked at the paper to see "Visual Information Production-Documentation Specialist." I had no idea what that meant and asked the personnel person about it. She said it had something to do with graphics and billboards, but that's all she knew about it. Once again, I thought to myself, *It could be worse,* so I was ready to just get to school and figure it out. Of course, as luck would have it, the school for this job wasn't there in Mississippi at Keesler Air Force Base; it was located on Lowry Air Force Base. I was headed to Colorado.

After I arrived at my dorm in Lowry, I soon discovered that my job was commonly referred to as "combat camera." And as the name suggests, my new school was to learn all facets of video production and broadcasting. Once I realized that, I was super excited and anxious to get started, although I had no idea how this job played a role in the air force. It seemed like it would be a fun job, and as it turned out, I ended up being very good at it.

School came and went, and I was very successful. I scored well on all my tests and found a natural comfort behind the console doing video postproduction. This consisted of taking all the raw footage that we had shot and editing it all together with music and effects to make it look fancy. I loved it. Not only did I love it, but the instructors loved what I was doing and chose me and another army student to edit our final class video. Much like with basic training, I found some much-needed validation of my self-worth that I had always been missing, and I remember it being nice to finally seem appreciated for all the good things I was capable of doing and could bring to the table. I never had any of that validation growing up, so things were really starting to change in my life and inside of me.

The air force was so good to me, and I wouldn't change a thing. The things I got to do, the places I got to see, and the things I got to experience during my twenty-three years are things I'll always be grateful for. You'll read more specifics about my career and those things as you go and about the woman I got to share most of it with too.

For I consider that the sufferings of this present time are not worth comparing with the glory that is to be revealed to us.

—Romans 8:18

CHAPTER 9

Misty and the Beginning of Parenthood

I met Misty (please note the spelling as a different "Misti" will enter the picture in a future chapter) at Patrick Air Force Base in 1994. I was engaged to Darci at the time; but as I said, she fell victim to the new me that was emerging, and the long-distance thing wasn't working out. It was inevitable that the relationship would end. Misty was beautiful, and she was the talk of our unit. Every guy in the unit was interested in her, including me.

As luck would have it, Misty ended up working just up the stairs from me in the same building I worked in. (Ironically, her job was actually the same one that I failed out of; and yes, she let me know often who the smart one was in our relationship.) She was waiting on getting her security clearance, so they put her upstairs in our command section with the secretary, doing paperwork until the security clearance was finalized and she could work in the base communications center. Our secretary, Jane, loved me, and I went up to visit her in her office often. It wasn't out of the ordinary for me to go visit her at least once per day, but at this point, I found myself having a brand-new and more exciting reason to go up to see her every day. And that's exactly what I did.

Misty was amazing, beautiful and smart, funny and athletic. She was a little piece of heaven in my world full of craziness as I had become popular and was getting so much attention I wasn't used to. Somehow, I got Misty's attention despite other people attempting to keep her away from me. As I mentioned previously, a new me was emerging—an arrogant one. I don't think I was nearly as bad when I met Misty as I would end up being later, but there was still an off-putting arrogance present, and it rubbed many people the wrong way. That's why many tried to keep her away from me; she had been warned.

Our romance started on the beach as we were both pretty good volleyball players. And being stationed in Cocoa Beach with the

THE SHELF

Atlantic Ocean just a short ten-second walk away from the front gate of the base, there was never a shortage of beach volleyball games to play. We would play at a local bar called "The Pier" after work some days, and because my circle of friends included those who had taken Misty in (we were all in the same unit), Misty joined us one day. That was when it was all over for me.

I'll never forget the first time I felt the "vibe" or knew that maybe she was interested in me. We were playing volleyball on the beach and were on opposite teams. I was in the front line in the center with my hands on my knees looking down at the sand. I remember starting to look up; and under the net, all I could see was the most amazing set of calves I'd ever seen on a woman. Of course, they ended up being Misty's, and a source of conversation for many, many years—even after we were married. She caught me looking, and with her beautiful blue eyes staring right at me, she flashed that smile at me that always made my heart melt. I knew then that maybe something significant was there. However, at this point in my life as a nineteen-year-old, it was about the challenge, not so much about love or a relationship, I'd come to learn about myself. Sad to say, but true nonetheless.

Misty and I spent a lot of time together after that. She didn't have a car when she first got there, so I would offer to take her to appointments and places she needed to go. We'd talk often and spend time together when we could. Because we worked so closely together, we'd often go to lunch together too. This was where the conversations turned from just flirting and casual to a little more serious and more substantial in nature.

I still remember one of our lunch dates at the base dining facility very clearly. Of course, being the oblivious and totally careless young man that I was, I continued to wear Darci's class ring even while talking to Misty. And Misty, being the ever-observant and brilliant woman she was, noticed. And then she asked. I played it off, of course, and made up something. I remember thinking at the time that I had probably just blown my chance with her.

With that lesson learned, the class ring came off, and that relationship from my past eventually ended for good shortly after—not because I had envisioned a future with Misty at this point, but because I just knew that this new life I was living was not conducive to settling down with one woman for the rest of my life. Don't get me wrong, though, it's not as if I didn't have feelings for Misty—I did. I just wasn't ready for a long-term relationship with the way my life was going at the time. But I had no idea at the time that I would end one relationship for that reason yet end up doing exactly what I didn't think I was ready for with Misty about a year later.

Our romance became well-known throughout our circle; and despite the warnings, Misty saw something in me that others never did. We started dating, and I wish I could tell you that it was all rainbows and unicorns, good times and true love. But it wasn't. Many times, I found ways to leave her, sabotage us, blame her, or lose interest in the challenge. I don't think anyone is naive to think that we didn't sleep together—we did, many times. But it just wasn't there for me at first; and when you're young and don't care the way you should, things like this happen. I'm not proud of that or how I treated her during that time either.

What followed was a whirlwind of new emotions, young love, and turmoil. It's much like what you've probably heard about or have gone through yourself: you get the girl (or guy), it's all cool and fun and exciting until it isn't, and then you don't really want to have much to do with them until you see them with someone else and realize that your feelings were probably stronger than you ever knew. And that's exactly what happened to me: jealously, emotions, fear, anxiety.

I didn't like it at all. I guess this was the point when I realized that there was more to it than I thought. This was the point when I thought maybe I truly loved her. We tried to deny it, but ultimately, there was no way to do that. It was there, and despite my earlier thoughts about not settling down, I didn't like how jealousy felt. It was the first time I had really felt that way. So I had to finally accept the fact that I loved Misty, and I needed to try. That's when something happened between us that would change my world forever and change everything about it that I had ever known before. Misty told me she was pregnant.

I've often joked with people over the years (even Misty) that the best twenty-seven months of our marriage was while she was pregnant. The first nine were no exception. I felt a love like I had never known as Misty and I experienced every kick, every ultrasound, every Lamaze class, and every unknown "first" together. Here were two young kids embarking on a new career in the air force, who were now about to add a child to that journey. It made us grow up fast. It gave us more than just ourselves to worry about. It was amazing and felt good. But still, I was me; and that me wasn't going away no matter how much I wanted it to.

The defining moment in our relationship came during the summer when she went home to New York (near where I grew up, as it would turn out) to visit her family. They knew about her being pregnant and supported her as any family would. We talked on the phone while she was gone, but we weren't in a good place, and the conversations we had weren't always happy the way they probably should've been. One night, during a conversation, she told me something that changed everything in me, though. She said, "I love you, David, but I have to think of our child first. And if that means I have to do this without you, then I will."

As you can imagine, that hit me hard. Flashes of my life and childhood ran through my brain, and I knew in that moment that I had found the woman whom I wanted to be the mother of my children, someone who would always put the children first before anything else, someone who would sacrifice her own desires for what was best for the children, someone who knew what true love was and could maybe teach me too. I told myself in that moment that I was *not* going to become my father; I was *not* going to abandon my child; I was *not* going to ever make her wonder if Daddy loved her or ever give her a reason to question my love, like I had with my own parents. I had a responsibility to this woman and my child, and I wouldn't allow myself to fail. I was on a new mission, having the sheer will and determination to never, ever be like my own father.

I don't remember exactly how the conversation ended, but I know she came back to Florida and things were better for us then. She had to move out of the dorms and into a house once she prepared for her pregnancy, and I spent as much time with her as I could, despite the air force saying that I couldn't stay there in her house and occupy a dorm room. Misty and I weren't married, so legally in the eyes of the air force, I couldn't stay in her house like I was. In fact, I got caught and almost got in trouble a few times for it. It wasn't easy, but we made it work.

Our firstborn, Logan Erin, was the most amazing thing that had ever happened to me in my life, a blessing and a true angel in disguise; she was perfect. The moments leading up to her birth were all amazing as Misty and I experienced all the "firsts" of pregnancy and childbirth together. From Lamaze classes to Misty's water breaking, I was there for it all. In fact, I'll never forget the day her water broke. I just happened to be near the base gate on a video job, so when I was finished, I ran out the gate to Misty's house to see how she was doing. I'll never forget her standing there on the phone with a friend of hers, and then *splash!* I can still see it to this day. We both looked down, and then at each other, and knew it was time.

By the time I got her to her doctor's office in Cocoa Beach, she was already at five centimeters dilated. I had gotten to her house around noon or so that day; we got to the doctor's office around one o'clock, and he told us to immediately go to Cape Canaveral Hospital because she was close to delivering. And at 3:22 in the afternoon on St. Patrick's Day, Logan was born, coming into the world at a perfect eight pounds and eight ounces and nineteen and a half inches. I cut the umbilical cord without hesitation after saying for months that I couldn't; and as Misty held Logan in her arms for the first time, I leaned over them and cried my eyes out. I still have the photo somewhere. This was the beginning of something brand-new; this was the beginning of something amazing; this was the beginning of my being a father and having a family.

I remember getting Logan home that first day. Misty and I sat on the couch and set the car seat down on the floor in front of us. As I set it down and sat down, Misty and I looked at each other and said, "What do we do now?" We had no idea; no idea where to start, no idea what to do or where to go. Sure, we had taken all the classes and read all the books, but in that moment, there were no answers. There was no handbook that would tell you what to do next. We were just two young unmarried teenagers with a day-old baby and no direction. It was crazy that one minute I was a single guy living a bachelor's life, and the next minute I was a father with a brand-new life I was now responsible for. Talk about getting a dose of reality and having to grow up really fast.

Misty and I really enjoyed life after Logan was born. Things had changed so much that our focus was no longer on our differences; it was on Logan. We had all those first-time parent things to do. It was new and exciting and scary all at the same time. We really didn't have time to worry about being young, dating other people, or any of the things that had come between us before.

After a while, it seemed like life was about as normal as it could be. We did the parent thing for a few months even though we weren't married yet and took Logan with us to all our picnics and gatherings and everything else we would do together. At this point, I decided it was time to make this little family complete as I was still having to live in the dorms, and I didn't like being apart from them (although I don't think I really missed much after Logan was born despite what the air force said I was allowed and not allowed to do). So I got a small engagement ring with what little money I made as a young airman in the air force and asked Misty to marry me. She said yes, of course; and less than four months later, we were married at a small ceremony on a wooden deck overseeing the Atlantic Ocean. Logan was still very little then, and while we may have done things backward in the eyes of most, I was happy that Logan was there with us on that day.

Finally, Misty and I could be together to raise our child and start our life and military careers together. And that's exactly what we did.

CHAPTER 10

My Career, Part 2

I remember one of my last days in school at Lowry as we were nearing graduation, and everyone was finding out where they'd get stationed next to do their jobs. It was quite an honor to finally be considered "permanent party," a term used for those people who had graduated from school and went on to a new base to start their career doing what they were trained to do.

As I said before, I was very naive to the air force and everything in it. I knew nothing about facing movements and saluting prior to basic training. In addition to that, I had no idea how many air force bases there were or where many of them were located. All I was hoping for at that point was that I'd get stationed at one of the two bases open in New York: Griffiss AFB and Plattsburgh AFB.

It was my turn. The person giving out the assignments was calling out names and bases and giving out our permanent change of station orders. All I heard was "Airman DeRemer...Patrick Air Force Base." That was followed by loud "oohs" and "ahs" from many of the other airmen in the room. I had no idea where I was headed or why these people were making noise about it, so I responded inquisitively, "Where is that?" Everyone looked shocked.

Apparently, I was about to go to a hidden little paradise of the air force known as Patrick Air Force Base located in Cocoa Beach, Florida. It was located on a barrier island on the east coast of Florida with the Atlantic Ocean on one side and the Banana River on the other. And as the conversation in the classroom ensued that day, I guess it was such an amazing location that I should have known about this paradise on earth prior to hearing I was getting stationed there.

Needless to say, I was excited about where I was headed. God had surely gotten me that far; and in that moment, I felt He was definitely being good to me, sending me to a place like that to start my career. I was excited to see what exactly He had in store.

Patrick Air Force Base didn't disappoint. You could go to the main gate, cross the street, and literally be on the beach overlooking the ocean. And when I say literally, I mean the ocean was not more than one hundred yards from the main gate. That was the hot spot for many of the local surfers, and there was daily action on the beach and in the water. It was a pretty awesome beginning of an adult life for a New York boy who hadn't had the opportunity to experience the world yet. This was the place where I would come into my own as an athlete, and also the place where I would meet my wife and have my first child as I've already talked about a little (you'll read more about all of that later).

I ended up being a very successful video production editor while stationed there, editing everything from unit mission videos to rocket and space shuttle launches. That success led to my earning many quarterly and annual awards and being named the 1996 Patrick Air Force Base Airman of the Year, 1996 Patrick Air Force Base Military Volunteer of the Year, and the Cocoa Beach Area Chamber of Commerce Service Award winner for 1996 and 1997.

I had so much success during my time at Patrick, and I felt I had finally found my place. After years of feeling inadequate and worthless, I was being noticed; I was being recognized; I was finding success. I was actually very, very good at all the things I was doing, both personally in sports as a four-sport athlete and professionally as a video producer, and people were noticing. God's hands were all over my life, and I had no idea He was preparing me for so much more at the time. So much was happening, and I was happy about it all. Career wise, life was good.

As I said earlier, Misty and I met, got married, and had Logan while I was at Patrick. The three of us left Patrick in November 1997 for Charleston Air Force Base. About six months prior to our departure, I had learned the air force had outsourced my job to civilian positions, and that I would be forced to relocate. Among my choices was Charleston Air Force Base, the place where my brother was stationed. Mark graduated from high school in 1994 and followed in big brother's footsteps and joined the air force after graduating, so it was an obvious choice to go to a base where we already knew someone, and the transition would be easier. Plus, we liked the nice weather, and spending a few more years in that climate was okay with us. Mark had already been to Florida to visit us and spend time with Logan, so when the day came for us to head to Charleston to be together again, we were all excited. I couldn't wait to be stationed with my brother because not many siblings get that chance in the military. And with our childhood history being what it was and our not growing up together, it allowed for our brotherly bond to grow as adults, something I've always been so grateful to God for allowing to happen.

We got to Charleston and ultimately spent seven years there. I ended up in the base multimedia center doing video production and had much of the same success as I had at Patrick. I was involved in sports and in-base events and knew everyone. Logan was growing up fast, and we were enjoying our life. My relationship with my brother was amazing, and Mark was able to watch Logan grow up too. It was great that she had so many years with her Uncle around. Of course, Jordan and Alli also came along while we were all at Charleston, so Uncle Mark got the chance to really enjoy his time with my kids and be there when they were born, another thing I'm grateful for. You'll read more about the kids later on in the book.

Mark met his current wife Melissa at Charleston, and I was able to help him plan his engagement and how he'd ask Melissa to marry him. It was great to be together for that too. It's pretty cool to look back now at all the different ways God worked in our lives that we didn't even realize at the time. I was a believer for sure back then but was also a huge hypocrite when it came to my faith. It didn't stop me from being thankful and feeling blessed though.

At that time, Mark wasn't a believer and didn't think there even was a God. Once I became a born-again Christian, got baptized, and truly knew God, I carried around a very heavy burden feeling as if the hypocrisy I had shown my brother was the cause of his not being a believer. All I knew to do later on in life as my faith matured was to let Mark see God through me, and that's exactly what I feel happened. It led to Mark's not only finding God, but in his own dedicated and selfless faith, Mark led me back to God when I had lost my way—truly bringing everything back full circle like you could never even imagine. For now, let's just say that the power of God is amazing and sometimes unbelievable. I've often had to pinch myself because of where His plan has led Mark and me now (more on that later too).

Charleston was good for me. I won many quarterly and annual awards while I was there, maintaining the "sustained excellence" that the air force required in order for us to get promoted. I was well on my way to a promising career with no hiccups up to that point. The only issue I had at that point in my life was my arrogance and my interpersonal skills with my peers and supervisors. Everyone else outside of my professional inner circle loved me. I had amazing relationships with members of other units, first sergeants, and even the squadron and wing commanders, but it was always my lack of interpersonal skills amongst those closest to me and my daily activities that was a problem. Maybe there was a reason for it.

In 1998, I was sent to Aviano Air Base in Italy. I spent four months there doing my job and enjoying everything about the beautiful country. I lived in an apartment that was paid for by the air force and had a sparkling new black Alfa Romeo with eight miles on it waiting for me outside my apartment when I arrived. I played basketball and lifted weights, and even played on a semipro Italian volleyball team for a short period of time. It was amazing.

As I was nearing the end of my tour in Italy, I got a call from one of my coworkers in Charleston and was told that when I got back, we were all moving to a different unit. On Charleston, our career field was unique in that you could be assigned to either the Communications Squadron's multimedia center, whose sole mission was to provide multimedia support to the base and base units, or be assigned to the Combat Camera Squadron, where we document deployed operations around the world. In other words, if there was a

THE SHELF

war going on, Combat Camera was there; if there was a humanitarian effort underway, Combat Camera was there; and if you wanted to be deployed and away from your family all the time, Combat Camera was the place to be.

Being gone all the time wasn't high on my list of things I wanted to do. Misty and I had just had Jordan, and I was just returning from Italy. Regardless, I knew I'd be sent out again soon after my return. I wasn't happy.

CHAPTER 11

Bosnia

It wasn't long after I moved to Combat Camera that I was sent out the door as I had anticipated would happen. First, it was a few weeks here and there to different forms of training. Then, I was notified I'd be deploying on a team to Bosnia to document the aftermath of the war in Sarajevo and also provide video support for the capture of any persons indicted for war crimes or PIFWCs as we called them.

These PIFWCs would generally be hiding to avoid capture; but at that time, US and coalition forces intel was actively searching. We had a top ten poster on our office walls even, with photos of the most wanted PIFWCs and the horrid crimes they were wanted for. From rapes to mass murders, all the crimes were gruesome and awful. If a PIFWC was captured, it was our job to document the apprehension, search, and transport of the prisoner to The Hague in the Netherlands to face charges at what used to be the International Criminal Tribunal for the former Yugoslavia. (A total of 161 people were indicted from 1991–2017 when the institution formally ceased to exist in December that year). I didn't learn about this part of the deployment until after we got there. And as "luck" would have it, they captured a couple while I was there (more on that later).

I prepared to leave for Bosnia, and it was hard. I had already missed so much. Jordy was only a month old when I left for Italy, and I missed Christmas that same year with her, Logan, and Misty. I didn't want to leave them, and at the time, nothing seemed fair. We all cried a lot that day. I was only home for a couple months from Italy before they sent me right back out again, and all I wanted to do was just stay home with my family. It was just the beginning of many, many years that Misty and I were separated from each other due to deployments, schools, and remote tours.

Bosnia was an eye-opener for me. I was new to the Combat Camera Squadron right before we left, so I didn't know the team of people I went with very well. They had all been friends for a while, and with the exception of the maintenance guy with us whom I was previously stationed with at Patrick, I didn't talk to any of the others much. In addition, a captain from another base was put in charge of our team, and none of us knew him either. So as you can imagine, the dynamic between us all wasn't ideal for what a true "team" should be.

The entire deployment was kind of a mess. I didn't get along well with the rest of the team, and I got caught up in some back and forth with them about various things. One of the female videographers and I didn't get along also, which led to much tension during our time there. Nothing major happened, but it just didn't make for an enjoyable time while we were there. The captain in charge was a real piece of work as he cared more about his display of naked women on his walls and dating any woman who'd give him a chance—this while he had a wife and children at home. I only mention that part because it's significant to the events that played out after we got back home to Charleston.

I got to experience many things in Bosnia. It was my first time in a war-torn country, giving me a true understanding of what had happened over there. It was a very different experience than the one I had in Italy. Bullet holes riddled almost every building. Restaurants, stores, and newspaper plants were nothing but piles of stone on the ground after being bombed. Kids roamed the streets looking for food and clothing. People lived in buildings with walls and windows blown out. It was incredible, and something I'll never forget.

We got home from Bosnia near the end of the year. If I remember correctly, it was right before Christmas. Many of the significant events that have happened in my life seemed to have happened near or around Christmas. You can draw your own conclusions as to why that is. Still today, while it's generally regarded as "the most wonderful time of the year," Christmas time sometimes reminds me of some of my most unhappy memories (I think you'll start to see that as you read more). Regardless, I was home and happy. My beautiful family of four was together finally, and we had no reason to think that we'd be separated again any time soon.

Not long after the new year had begun and we got comfortable being a family, Misty received news that she was going on a remote tour to South Korea. Remote tours mean unaccompanied without your family. It's the one thing you know is going to happen at least once in your career, but hope the day never comes. For Misty, it did and at a time when I had just returned from a couple of back-to-back deployments right beforehand. Again, we were going to be separated, and we had already begun to have issues as you'll read about later. It's really no wonder that our marriage and relationship didn't have time to grow. With my own personal issues, coupled with us constantly being separated, I think we were set up to fail from the start. As unfortunate as it is to say, our careers definitely played a factor in our divorce. Many people who are military-married-to-military will likely understand.

Misty was gone, and life for Logan, Jordy, and I went on. I absolutely loved my life with them and all the moments we shared together when they were little. Logan started kindergarten while Misty was gone, and Jordy was starting to walk and talk more. I was still playing sports and involved in many things. Looking back, I wish I had done things a little differently. Hindsight is always 20/20 when your kids are grown and gone, but I wish I hadn't carted them around to neighbors and my brother all the time to go play in my games whatever sport I happened to be playing at the time. I was young and still active; but above all else, I was arrogant and still wanted to be the center of attention. I was very misguided in that way.

My career was blossoming, and I was making a name for myself, but my personal life and interpersonal skills were lacking. My arrogance was an issue for many people, including Misty. It was an issue long before we left Patrick and was still an issue at Charleston. At times, all I think I cared about was myself. I had gone from being a worthless kid who was told he'd never make anything of himself, to a successful young airman and athlete who ended up being very good at the things I never knew I was good at. It went to my head. I went from one end of the spectrum to the other, from having no self-esteem to being totally arrogant and flaunting it all. And because of the sudden change, I didn't know how to respond to it all very well. I just knew I liked it. I liked being good at something; I liked that everyone saw it. And the more success I found, the worse my arrogance got.

A little while after Misty left for Korea, I got a message at the squadron that I needed to report to a building for an interview. No one would tell me what it was about, but I had heard rumors that the captain who was with us in Bosnia was being investigated for a few different things that happened while we were all in Bosnia. Other than the naked photos on the wall in his room and his constant flirting and talking to other women, I didn't know much and was never really involved in the things he did like the others were. One of the guys with us in charge of our combat camera team was actually the captain's roommate, so he saw more than any of us did. But even that guy had an alcohol problem, was a terrible leader, and didn't know the meaning of the word "work." Unfortunately for us airmen, we had zero leadership while we were in Bosnia, and it would come back to haunt me specifically—and unknowingly—on this day.

I walked into the office and was abruptly told to sit down by an officer behind the desk. He was totally unprofessional and rude to me and treated me like dirt. I remember thinking that no one had ever talked to me or treated me like that before, and I was starting to sense that something was very, very wrong here. I assumed I was there to answer questions about the captain and what I had experienced with him while in Bosnia, but what followed when that guy started talking was something I never saw coming.

Suddenly, I go from thinking I'm being interviewed about what I had witnessed in Bosnia to being read my rights and accused of three different violations of the Uniform Code of Military Justice to include simple assault, indecent language, and failure to obey a direct order.

As you can imagine, I was totally caught off guard and in shock. These charges were serious, and I knew that if found guilty, it would result in serious consequences and ruin my career. Again, I was in shock. I had no idea where any of this was coming from or why I was the one being accused of it all. Once the initial shock wore off, I just wanted answers. But I had seen enough *Law & Order* episodes in my day to know that I shouldn't say anything until I had spoken to my own lawyer. I knew not to say any more other than asking a few times "Me?" and "Are you sure you have the right person?"

I had educated and mentored many of my airmen on that very thing—to utilize the resources available to them, when and if it was ever necessary—so while I knew I had done nothing wrong and wanted to know more right then, I didn't say any more. And I didn't want to talk to this guy anymore anyway. He treated me like I was already found guilty of these things. I just said I wanted to speak to a lawyer, left that office and immediately visited the Area Defense Counsel's office where the lawyers made available to us in times like these were located.

As it turned out, when we returned from Bosnia, many of the people on our team began talking to others in our unit about the captain and all the things that happened while we were there. There were many rumors that floated around for a couple months after our return, and it wasn't until these rumors made their way to our chain of command that someone looked into it. And from what I would soon find out, mine was the name that came out of everyone's mouth in very coordinated stories. To believe it, you would've had to live it. It was something straight out of a movie—when someone is wrongly accused, but everyone else is singing the same song and there's nothing you can do about it because you're the only one telling your side of the story. I was new to the unit, on a team with a bunch of people who were all friends and had been in the unit for years, and no one knew me or the stellar career I had up to that point. None of that mattered. Nothing I had accomplished before that mattered. I was stuck.

After a couple hours, I was finally able to get the information from my lawyer. The simple assault charge was for allegedly touching the buttocks of the female airman I didn't get along with, who also did video on our team; the indecent language charge was for a lewd comment that was made with regard to the provocative clothes that same female would wear while running on the treadmill; and the failure to obey a direct order charge was for my allegedly not following a direct order to stop sexually harassing the same female. I had no idea what was going on.

There are many details to share about this situation that happened over the course of the next two years. Story after story swirled around the unit and the entire base about what was happening. You see, I had already started to make a name for myself on the base, so leadership all the way up to the base commander was in shock. However, with combat camera being what they call a "tenant unit," the base chain of command who really knew me had no say in anything that happened because our unit fell under a different group and wing located in New Jersey. I was helpless. No one believed a word that I said, and all the people in high places who knew me and knew I wouldn't do the things I was accused of couldn't do anything about it.

My lawyer wasn't much help, so I knew that if I was going to clear my good name, I had to get to work. I was offered an Article 15 punishment, which was the commander's informing me of the alleged offenses I was accused of, his giving me a few days to respond, and then the commander's looking at all the information and my response and deciding what to do—whether it be to drop the whole thing or give punishment.

Immediately following this meeting, I went to work on the failure to obey a direct order charge. I knew none of the things I was accused of ever happened except for one (more on that later), so obviously I was never given a direct order to stop anything. Remember the guy in charge of our team who had an alcohol problem? He was the one who supposedly gave me the order. I confronted him, and he wasn't expecting it. He buckled easily when standing face to face with me; and at this point, I had nothing to lose and *zero* fear. There was no proof of any such order, and I was told he backtracked later after that when I told the first sergeant all about it. I was optimistic at this point as that was one of three charges now gone, and I had hardly begun to fight yet. And since I knew that I had done nothing wrong, I was sure it would all be taken care of soon after that.

Because I wasn't comfortable working in that squadron any longer, I asked to be permanently assigned back to the Communications Squadron multimedia center where I had started working when I first got to Charleston. The Communications Squadron first sergeant was my mentor; and after speaking to the combat camera first sergeant about my request, my old first sergeant wanted me back there. In a matter of hours, he made it happen. I was so thankful to be out of that environment, and when I got to my old first sergeant's office, the first thing out of his mouth was "What the hell is going on over there?"

Master Sergeant Brian Sommerfeldt was his name. I can safely say that if it wasn't for him, I wouldn't be where I am today. He was a former cop in the air force and pretty hardcore, but he really took to me, mentored me, and always took care of me. He was the type of leader you want, one who's a bulldog to those who wrong you, but a role model to follow who would set you up to succeed if he saw the good in you. This is how Brian was with me. He'd be the first one to call me and set me up with an opportunity that might help my career, but he'd also be the mentor that would kick my butt back in line when I needed it, and he did both often.

I told him everything that day. And for the first time, when all was said and done, I truly felt as if I had someone on my side. He believed me, supported me, and did everything he could to help me after that. And I was going to need all the help I could get too.

Dressed in full service dress three days after being offered my Article 15, I returned to the commander's office, snapped to atten-

THE SHELF

tion, saluted, and reported in. The commander was out due to some medical issues, so the deputy commander was the one there that day. There were so many inconsistencies like this during the entire process, with new people who weren't involved suddenly entering into the equation and making decisions, to all the stories changing from everyone except from me. There was no way that any of this could ever stand with all the craziness going on with it.

Boy was I wrong. I'd come to find out later on that the commander said he was going to make an example out of the new guy no matter what was said or done, and that was obvious as the punishment was handed down. Keep in mind, I was a Staff Sergeant-select (E-5) at the time; meaning, I had qualified for promotion (four stripes) but wasn't wearing it yet. So officially at that time, I was a senior airman (E-4) wearing three stripes.

My punishment was as follows: reduction in grade to E-2 (rank of Airman—one stripe), with a suspended bust to E-1 (rank of Airman Basic—no stripes) for six months, and forfeiture of one half month's pay for three months. (Suspended bust means you can be busted down again to E-1 if there are any other issues within six months of the punishment).

As some of my communications squadron and wing staff leaders said soon after they had heard the news, it was one of the greatest travesties ever. Not only did the punishment not fit the alleged crimes, the proof just wasn't there to justify the punishment either. Again, I was in complete shock.

Everyone on base knew me. Suddenly, I was a one-stripe airman walking around the base to curious onlookers and people whispering. My reputation was tarnished. My pay was cut by more than half. I was completely embarrassed and ashamed. And on top of all that, I was a dad taking care of two daughters on my own through all of it and now had to call and tell my wife, who was thousands of miles away in South Korea, what had just happened.

It wasn't easy after that. Misty didn't respond very well, and while she supported me on the surface, I'm sure she wondered what the truth really was. Anyone would, I guess. I felt bad that I was putting her in that situation too, but I knew I was innocent and had done nothing wrong. I had many faults but was never that type of guy. And now, I was on a mission to prove that I wasn't.

I could write a separate book about all that happened in the next two years. I did everything I could to prove my innocence. I became an expert on air force regulations and the law. I spent countless hours and sleepless nights doing research, reading books, and doing everything I could to make this right again. I had a family and a career at stake.

I talked to many people about the things I had seen in the final report of findings. The investigator had interviewed as many as twenty-five people in our unit, and many of them either didn't know me or didn't have very nice things to say. Some of the comments were strictly opinion, and some of the comments were just flat-out lies. Some people were caught off guard when I actually confronted them as I'm sure they didn't think I would ever find out what they had said or thought I'd never have the nerve to confront them. Many flat out denied saying certain things, and others said that their words were misinterpreted and portrayed as something they weren't meant to be and taken out of context. After getting this same reaction from a few different people, I began to dig further into the final report of findings. It didn't take much digging for me to soon discover that something seemed a little off. And after talking to people and reading the report hundreds of times, it finally hit me: this final report consisted the investigator's account of what the witnesses had said and not actual witness statements themselves. This was the same guy who treated me so poorly in the very beginning. Something wasn't right, and I was going to figure it out.

I had done enough research and sacrificed enough time with my girls to know that when someone is accused of something, they're supposed to be provided with all the evidence used against them. After talking to so many people and getting conflicting stories about what they said in their statements and what the final report said, I requested that the legal office and the investigator provide me with the original witness statements as written by the actual witnesses themselves.

At first, I had my lawyer request them. After a few days, I was told that they were looking for them and would get them to me as soon as they found them. A week or two later, after asking again, I was told the same thing. Finally, after about a month or so of waiting, I was tired of being given the runaround and took matters into my own hands.

Each base has what's called an inspector general. This is a high-ranking officer who runs the IG office where complaints are filed about many serious things such as complaints against commanders, racism, sexual harassment, hostile work environments, etc. It's generally considered a last resort when the chain of command is either involved or hasn't been able to help with a problem. Filing an IG complaint launches a big investigation and puts a huge spotlight on the individuals and the units involved. It's a serious thing, and if an IG complaint is lodged by someone, it's taken very seriously. It's the one thing that people don't want to see happen.

I went right to the inspector general myself and sat down in his office. He was a full bird Colonel and very impartial, just as he should have been. It was the first time in the entire process that I felt someone was actually listening other than my first sergeant Brian, who always took care of me. I talked to him and filed two complaints that day. The first complaint I filed was a claim that I was not provided with all the evidence used against me. The second complaint was a claim that there was false and misleading information in the report, leading the commander to make decisions based on inaccurate facts.

Now, to have a complaint come back substantiated by the IG is a big deal. It rarely happens unless there is very clear and overwhelming evidence of a wrongdoing. But when it does happen, it generally means that the person being wronged, if looking to overturn a punishment, has a huge piece of evidence to support making that happen. I didn't know what the colonel would find when he talked to people, but I knew that I had to do everything I could to prove my innocence, and this was my next course of action.

To make a long story short, I received a letter from the IG office about a month later. The colonel substantiated my first claim that I was not provided with all the evidence used against me. That was huge. Even my first sergeant Brian said that he was surprised I wasn't crying my eyes out after getting the IG findings letter because it was such a huge thing for me and my case. The colonel could not substantiate my second claim of there being false and misleading information used against me in the report; however, that actually helped my case more than it hurt it. You see, the witness statements were never found. Apparently, after it was known that I was requesting to see them and not the paraphrased final report written by the investigator, the witness statements all disappeared, never to be found again. Coincidence? I guess we'll never know. But the colonel couldn't substantiate my second complaint because he couldn't find the actual witness statements to verify if indeed the information in the report was false and misleading. So while he couldn't substantiate the complaint, the mere appearance of impropriety and mishandling of these important and key documents did more damage than the substantiated IG complaint ever could. (The investigator was eventually fired.)

At this point, I had cause to ask for my punishment to be set aside by the commander due to injustice. Being set aside means that the commander can right the wrong and restore the person punished back to where they were before the injustice occurred. This is only allowed if there is new evidence to provide that wasn't included prior to the punishment being served.

With my newly-substantiated IG complaint, I put together my set aside package and submitted it to my Communications Squadron commander. I didn't care for him much, and he didn't really know me. The commander I had there when I first got to Charleston was gone when I moved back there, and this new commander was a real piece of work that no one liked. Not even Brian, the commander's first sergeant and my friend. However, he was the one in the position, and I had no choice but to present it to him and hope for the best.

As it turned out, my request for set aside was denied. I'd find out later that my Communications Squadron commander was good friends with the Combat Camera Squadron commander who administered my punishment initially, so there was no way he was going to overturn the decision of his friend. Once again, I was just in the wrong place at the wrong time.

Other than feeling like I was fighting a losing battle, life was chugging along. The girls and I were doing good despite Misty's being gone, and I loved my job and loved being back in the Communications Squadron where everyone knew me, believed in me, and supported me through my tough times. I continued to do all the things I had done prior, both personally and professionally, and tried not to let the adversity get to me. I was still fighting to clear my name but was continuing on with life as normal.

That year would end up being good to me as I won two more Airman of the Quarter awards and another Airman of the Year award. It's funny to think about now. In 1996, I was a Senior Airman Three-Striper Airman of the Year at Patrick. And five years later in 2001, I was an Airman First Class Two-Striper Airman of the Year at Charleston. It was a crazy story to tell over the years to those who asked when those people would see the plaques on my office walls, and I'd see the confused look on their faces. I've never hidden my past; it's part of my story and helped make me the leader I am today. My experiences, both good and bad, have made me who I am. I've been at the very top, and I've been at the very bottom, and you just can't ask for better experience than that.

This is where the story takes quite a different turn. Because of how long I had been in the air force at this time, and due to my reduction in rank and the time it would take me to make rank back again, I was about to hit high year tenure. This meant that I would be forced to separate from the air force. It was a tough situation to be in as I had been so successful and was really on track to fast burn up the ranks. But I had exhausted all my options to get relief and change things, and there was nothing else left that I could do.

A short time went by and I was really starting to feel lost. I didn't know what the future was going to look like or what I would do next. I was married with kids; and suddenly, my career was about to be ripped away from me. I had never thought to do anything else from the time I was in junior high. The military was all I had known; the military gave me a life.

I'd lie in bed at night praying for guidance, trying to figure out what I could do next. For two years, I had sacrificed so much time with my girls working on my defense, and I couldn't just quit and have all my efforts and sacrifices be for nothing. Misty had already come back from Korea, and we were dealing with things. I just prayed and prayed and prayed. It was all I knew how to do at the time. Everything else I had done hadn't made a difference. Everyone who believed in me had no power to change anything, so I turned to God and let Him have all of it. I laid all my troubles, fears, and worries at His feet. And when I was finally able to do that, that's when He went to work.

I'll never forget the night that God's voice became clear. During all the time that had passed since Bosnia and all the time I had spent fighting this fight, I didn't once speak to the girl who had allegedly filed these complaints against me. I was advised not to speak to her; and honestly, I didn't really want to. In my mind, she was a liar, and the hostility I felt inside needed to stay inside. Confronting her would likely do more harm than good. I never understood why she'd lie, and I often wanted to get answers, but I knew that was never likely to happen, so I didn't think about it much. At least, not until that night.

I was lying in bed, praying for guidance like I had for so many nights before that. This night was different, though, as I started having these strong feelings that I needed to talk to that girl. I couldn't shake it. The feelings were so strong that my mind was flooded with questions and things to say—so much so that I grabbed the closest thing to me that I could write on and started writing everything down. It was a giant phone book with the back cover half torn off, and I was writing down everything that popped into my head on the yellow pages that were showing.

The next day, I took that phone book into work with me and sat down at my computer. Nervous and worried, but running out of hope, I just started typing. Everything I had written down the night before and all the thoughts I had to go along with them, I typed into this e-mail. And when I finally finished typing and read it all over, I knew exactly what I was supposed to do with it: I was supposed to send it all to that girl.

My anxiety was at an all-time high, of course, as I was anticipating the worst. I figured a response from combat camera leadership or my first sergeant, telling me that I wasn't allowed to talk to her anymore or that I needed to stop harassing her, was imminent. But

THE SHELF

I felt like this was what I was supposed to do, and my feelings were strong about doing it. I felt I had done a great job at taking the emotion out of the e-mail and really just focused on reality and truth so as not to create any hostility. I was hoping for a miracle, one that would help her see that the lies not only affected my career but also affected my children, my wife, and was taking its toll on my marriage. I just wanted to believe that if she had any heart at all, she would do something or say something to help me.

Well, I got way more than I ever bargained for. Over a year had passed at this point, and prior to feeling God's presence the night before, I had no intentions of talking to this girl—ever. That was my plan; God's plan was different.

I got an e-mail back from the girl, and despite its being such a public ordeal and affecting my life so much, she said she had no idea the gravity of what had happened, didn't know how badly I had gotten punished, and felt that things got blown way out of proportion. I was shocked. I wasn't quite sure just how much of what she said—about her ignorance to it all—was actually the truth, but I was going to take whatever I could get.

During the course of our correspondence, I discovered that people had been gossiping throughout the squadron since our team returned from Bosnia, she had given her statement to the investigator also and knew others had too, but she had no idea what had ever come of it. She said that she never accused me of doing anything and didn't know I was in trouble for any of it. While she did still contend that her buttocks got touched, and I was near her at the time, she said that it was dark, and she could never say for sure who did it or if she wasn't just brushed up against by accident. In addition to that, with regard to the indecent language allegation, she said she couldn't remember who made the comments and claimed she had never told anyone that it was me. I actually knew the comments had been made, and I also knew who had made them. It was probably the only thing that was actually true in this whole situation. However, what wasn't true was that I was the person who made them.

So I had already proved one allegation was false before even being punished, and now I had this new evidence that may help me clear my name once and for all. It all seemed so obvious to me, and these e-mails, coupled with my substantiated IG complaint letter and the witness statements conveniently disappearing, would be enough. I just knew it would be enough. I was in tears as I sat in my editing chair reading all of this from her and thinking, *Thank you, Lord, for this. This is really going to change everything.*

I'll just finish this story by saying that God was very present in me during this time. He renewed my faith in Him as I dealt with this for so long. I became a better man after this, a humbler man. And while I still needed so much work, this situation changed me.

Ultimately, it all happened on God's timing. The old squadron commander who denied my previous set aside request was now gone, and a new commander—one whom my first sergeant Brian had already told everything to—was now in place. I had new evidence to support my claims of innocence and now had a new, unbiased commander to review it all with a fresh set of eyes. Two years of fighting, two years of sleepless nights, two years of burying my head in legal books and air force regulations. I gathered up everything I had and submitted my set aside package to the new commander. It was all I had left; it was my last chance. And then I waited.

Finally, the day came, and the commander called me into his office. He apologized to me for all that I had been through and for the clear injustice I had suffered. Then he told me he had made a decision; he decided he was going to set aside my punishment. All the blood, sweat, tears, and sacrifices—they were all worth it.

I got all my stripes back. I was restored back to senior airman with all the appropriate dates of rank. I was also allowed to test for staff sergeant again. Because I had missed testing during those two years, my test scores were submitted and compared to the promotion scores for the two years prior. And after computing the results, they discovered that I would've gotten promoted the year prior. So not only did I get my original three stripes back, I was also promoted to staff sergeant and given a date of rank for the year prior. In addition to that, I received over ten thousand dollars in back pay for the difference in what I was paid during those two years and what I was supposed to have been paid as a senior airman and then as a staff sergeant.

THE SHELF

It was amazing on so many levels. I was vindicated; I was relieved; I was happy. It was a learning experience for sure, and one that I carried with me for the rest of my career. The system actually worked, and I was proof that if you fight for what you know is right, everything will eventually work out. Again, I had been at the very top and then at the very bottom, and those types of experiences can truly help you relate to everyone as a leader. I'm just glad that I kept the faith. While I haven't always been perfect in my faith, I have always been one to run toward God in times of adversity versus running away from Him and blaming Him. If I hadn't let go and let Him take over that night, it's likely I would have never talked to that girl and probably would be telling a very different story today—if I'd be telling one at all.

CHAPTER 12

My Career, Part 3

Our time at Charleston presented many challenges, but we made it through. I made many friends and got to do many things. I was blessed to have two more children there; it was the first time I had become a homeowner and even bought my first minivan, which I said I'd never own. Yes, kids change everything.

In keeping with our family separation tradition, I ended up getting my own unaccompanied assignment to South Korea in 2013. This forced me to leave my family again for a year at the end of 2003; and again, it was difficult. It was a long year apart.

In 2004, I went directly from Osan Air Base in South Korea to Kadena Air Base in Okinawa, Japan. Misty and the kids joined me a month after I got there. It was an amazing experience for all of us. Misty and I were both successful in our jobs, and both played softball and traveled all over the island and Korea. The girls were going to school on base and were fully immersed in the Okinawan culture, taking Japanese partial immersion classes every year and loving it. I'm so thankful for the opportunity to give my girls that experience, one they still talk about and share with others today.

Professionally, I was on the fast track for promotion after having all my rank restored and getting everything back to normal while at Charleston. I was a staff sergeant at Kadena and had tested for technical sergeant (E-6, five stripes) twice, missing it the last time by thirteen points. However, after reviewing my records once the promotion results came out, I discovered that there was one last piece of the past that was still lingering in my records. An old performance report was still in my records from my time at combat camera. This report had an unfavorable overall rating, and that rating was affecting the scores I needed to get promoted.

Understanding the performance report process isn't easy. For ease of understanding, I'll try to explain it here, so you fully understand the impact this was having on my career at this point. Performance reports were given annually and had seven different rated categories on the front side. Each category had four blocks going from left to right. Early on in my career, the blocks went from "inefficient" all the way to the left to "the exception" all the way to the right. Later in my career when the performance reports were revamped, the blocks changed to "does not meet" all the way to the left to "clearly exceeds" all the way to the right and was meant to be a rating of individual performance standards in the seven different categories over the course of that particular year or rating period.

The overall ratings of performance reports were on the back of this form, and everyone was rated on a scale of 1–5. Each overall rating was given a corresponding score toward promotion. The difference between a "5" overall rating and a "4" overall rating was very significant. These ratings could impact your promotion scores by anywhere from ten to fifty points, depending on the all of the ratings of the last ten reports you had during your career, if you had that many. So if you had ten reports, and each one was rated a "5," you received 135 points maximum toward promotion. If you had a poor performance report (or more than one) in your records during that time, you'd receive less points, and that would obviously impact your chances to reach the cutoff scores needed to get promoted. Again, getting a "4" instead of a "5" was a big difference. And the overall rating I got in my report after receiving my Article 15 punishment was a "2."

As I'd soon discover after some digging, removing performance reports was not part of the set aside process, and the commander does not have the authority to remove a report from a member's records. This is why my report during that time was never removed from my records like I thought it would be when my punishment was set aside. I found out that if someone wanted to have a report removed from their records, they had to appeal to the Air Force Board for Correction of Military Records, which was a difficult and often lengthy process. I didn't know that, so that "2" performance report was still in my records both times I had tested to get those five stripes. However, because the entire punishment had been set aside, it was justification enough for me to appeal to the board and have the poor performance report removed from my records.

Over the course of several months, I put together everything I needed to submit the appeal. Once I did, it took some time to hear back. When I finally did, the appeals board sent me a letter saying they had granted my appeal and, by order of the Secretary of the Air Force, removed the "2" performance report from my records.

Of course, my work didn't end there. Now that the report had been removed, I had to appeal to the same board again in order to have my test scores recalculated for the two years prior that I had tested for technical sergeant with that old report in my records. And with that report removed, my scores for promotion went up by thirty points, and I had only missed getting promoted the year prior by thirteen points. In other words, when they recalculated the scores as they should have been the year before, I had surpassed the score needed to get promoted. So after all that had happened over the previous few years, I was subsequently promoted to technical sergeant on the spot with the appropriate date of rank and all the back pay that came with it.

THE SHELF

After a few years struggling, I was finally back to the same place I was before. My career was back on track, and I couldn't have been happier. Not only was I happy to have all my stripes back, but happy to know that all of my hard work, efforts, and sacrifices were worth it. And shortly after that, I would test for master sergeant (E-7, six stripes) for the first time and get promoted the first time. Now, not only was I back on track, I was starting to pull ahead of my peers and move one step closer to that pinnacle of enlisted ranks, chief master sergeant (E-9, eight stripes).

In November 2008, we moved to Scott Air Force Base in Illinois. I worked in the base multimedia center at first, supporting the base units like I had in the past. At the tail end of my time at Kadena, the air force was starting to make major changes; and because of our similar missions, the air force decided to restructure all multimedia offices and merge the video, photo, graphics, and journalist career fields and put them all under the public affairs umbrella. So instead of being a multimedia center assigned to a communications squadron, we were now all just called public affairs assigned to the wing staff and considered a wing staff agency.

I worked as the section chief of video production during my time at Scott. We supported the base and also the headquarters since Scott Air Force Base was also home to Air Mobility Command Headquarters, the command our base fell under. In late 2009, I received orders to Afghanistan, with a couple months of combat training prior to that. It was another difficult time as I found myself once again going to be gone for Christmas. And this by far was going to be my most dangerous deployment yet.

It wasn't exactly the place I wanted to go with sixteen years in the air force and only a few more to go before retirement. However, the air force's needs always came first, and I went. I ended up being the superintendent of the Public Affairs Advisory Team, whose mission was to train Afghan soldiers on all public affairs functions in order to counter false and misleading messages being broadcasted to civilians by the Taliban. It was an interesting six months, and I'm not sure we had much of a lasting impact on the Afghan soldiers. Many of the advisory teams had disbanded because of it. The government and military leaders were just too corrupt, and no amount of training was going to change that, in my opinion.

For the most part, it seemed as if the Afghan soldiers cared more about what Americans could buy for them and give them than they ever did about being trained and using that training to actually make a difference. I did what I could while I was there. I saw beheadings and some gruesome things. One of the Afghan soldiers I was training ended up leaving the army to join the Taliban. We found all of his uniforms and equipment left behind in a bathroom one day. It was a crazy place, and the culture was just very different.

In my heart, I knew that my efforts were being wasted, and the time away from home wasn't worth it. On the surface and in the news, it may have seemed like Americans occupying that territory was helpful, but it really wasn't. As someone who was there, I can honestly say, in my opinion, we wasted every dollar and every ounce of our efforts while we were there. And if that was any indication of what the big picture was for others who were in the same position, it's no wonder why we still have issues over there today. I'm not sure I even have an answer for what could be done differently. And I know our leaders are making the best decisions they can with what they know. Sometimes, the best decisions don't necessarily give you the results you want or expect, and maybe this was a fight that we shouldn't have been involved in to begin with.

THE SHELF

I returned from Afghanistan and was given an opportunity to become a first sergeant for the wing staff agencies and comptroller squadron at Scott Air Force Base. I was pretty excited about the opportunity, knowing the impact that my first sergeant Brian had had on my career during the difficult time I went through in combat camera. I wanted to have that sort of impact on others; and as a natural leader who loved taking care of airmen, that's exactly what I would end up doing.

I was a first sergeant for a year before being provided yet another opportunity that would set me up for success and promotion. I was selected by command to attend the Public Affairs Officer Qualification Course, where only a select few senior noncommissioned officers were able to attend. Of course, I was in the first sergeant position at the time and absolutely loved what I was doing, but this was an opportunity I had to take. Eventually, I knew I would have to go back to my career field, and I wanted to take advantage of this course that would really help me rise above my peers and help me stand out on the senior master sergeant (E-8, seven stripes) promotion board coming up. So off to school I went.

I spent a few months at Fort Meade, Maryland, at the Defense Information School where members from all military services, along with civilians, were trained on everything that had to do with military communications from video, photo, and graphics to journalism, media preparation, officer leadership courses, and everything in between. It's the Department of Defense's premier schoolhouse for training the military how to communicate the mission to the world.

I learned a lot while I was there as my school was pretty advanced and taught me how to do an officer's job as an enlisted member. Of course, I had many years of experience in the career field already, but this school and the advanced training provided filled many of the gaps I needed to be fully prepared to lead in the public affairs field. As a senior leader, I needed to know these things to be credible when overseeing a public affairs office as a superintendent, the job I always wanted, and one I was hoping my command would vector me toward.

I returned to Scott Air Force Base after school and moved from the base multimedia center to command headquarters where I was in charge of social media strategy and management for the command and the thirteen subordinate bases that fell under the command. I had the opportunity to learn more about the mission of the command and also about the missions of each of our bases in the command. At this point in my career, it was the job I needed to see a more strategic picture of how things were run at that level and fully understand why senior leaders made the decisions they did. Again, it was another piece of the puzzle I needed to be fully prepared to lead an entire public affairs unit, which I would end up doing in my very last job in the air force before retirement.

My career, while difficult and unorthodox at times in how I got there, took a pretty textbook path with regard to career vectoring and progression. It all culminated into my becoming a public affairs superintendent overseeing the entire operation, the place most of us career-minded PA enlisted folks strove to get to. It's a pretty cool story to tell, and I definitely didn't take a straight line from point A to point B to get there, that's for sure. But I wouldn't change a thing now, and you'll read more about my final position as a superintendent—and my extraordinary and spiritual experiences at Luke Air Force Base—later on in the book.

Now as I wind down this chapter on my career, I think it's important to point out something that you may not have realized already. Or if you're incredibly observant and have had the ability to truly follow the story line so far, you may already know what's coming next.

I started out talking about when I joined the air force, leaving for basic training, and going to school. If you remember, I talked about how I went in thinking I had a guaranteed job in public affairs, but when I got to basic training, I found out that I didn't have a guaranteed job and ended up being sent to Keesler Air Force Base to go to school to be a communications computer systems operator. I ended up failing out of that job and was then sent to Lowry Air Force Base to go to school to be a visual information production and documentation specialist, or a videographer and combat cameraman. As my career progressed and the years went by, you heard about the air force restructuring and realigning our career fields and ultimately changing multimedia into public affairs.

It's funny how things work out when you really think about it. I joined the air force, thinking I had a guaranteed job in public affairs—I didn't. I ended up going to school for a completely different job instead, I ended up failing out of that job, and I then went to school to be a videographer. And eventually, the video, photo, and graphics career fields would end up merging with the journalist career field; and ultimately, all would become what is now known as Air Force Public Affairs. It all came full circle, didn't it? God is pretty amazing, isn't He?

CHAPTER 13

My Girls

One of the greatest gifts that God ever game me was the opportunity to be a father. And not only did He bless me that opportunity once, He blessed me with it three times in the form of the three most perfect human beings I could have ever asked for.

You've already heard a little bit about my oldest daughter. Logan Erin was born on St. Patrick's Day (March 17th) in 1995 in the early afternoon at Cape Canaveral Hospital in Florida. She was a beautiful eight pounds and eight ounces and came complete with a big set of lungs and a crooked little nose. As first-time parents, Misty and I were truly happy and emotional about having a baby and were excited about being parents and all growing together. I had just received an absolutely amazing gift from God. I was blessed with "My Angel."

I can still remember all the little things—her first word ("da da," of course), her first time rolling over, her first steps, and eating real food for the first time. She was always such a happy and good baby. Misty worked a crazy schedule at times, so it was always an interesting dynamic to be new parents and figure out all the best ways to do everything for her.

My favorite moments early on were bedtime. She was always smiling and happy; and at bedtime, she was always really cuddly and sweet. But it wasn't always easy to get her to go to sleep. One night, I had music playing, and the song "Endless Love" by Lionel Richie came on. Logan immediately calmed down and fell asleep on my chest in the rocking chair. I remembered thinking that maybe there was a little something to it, so I tried it the next night too. She'd lay on my chest in the rocking chair; and if the CD wasn't playing, I'd just sing it to her. It almost brings tears to my eyes as I write this as I can still see her little face looking up at me as she lay there on my chest, her eyes getting heavy as she would quickly drift away into a peaceful sleep. Those are the type of moments you just never forget as a parent, and the moments that always seem to go by too fast.

Misty and I had been through all the Lamaze classes together and had a midwife who would come to the house at various stages of Logan's life to show us things and help us learn everything we needed to know as new parents. Looking back now, I feel so lucky to have had the support we did from so many people and thankful we had so many military resources available to us to make our first-time parenting experience easier.

I still remember Logan's first time eating real food. We had her in her car seat on top of the dining room table. Her little face was so cute as she took that first spoonful (carrots, I believe it was). It was a pretty normal response—the "what is this?" face followed by the smacking of lips and spitting it out all over the place. Of course, it wasn't spitting it out because she didn't like it as much as it was that she just didn't know what else to do with it! After a couple tries, she finally figured it out, and we had taken the next step in raising our child and helping her grow up.

Through the years, we got Logan into everything. She played sports, she was a girl scout, and she was a cheerleader. She loved cheering, and that would be what she'd do the most during her younger days. Misty would coach her team, and she was very good at it. Misty and Logan won many cheerleading awards together, and I was the supportive dad who lost his voice screaming all the time. It was the niche that Logan found, one that she loved and was very good at.

The one thing I love the most about my girls is that each one has their own very distinct and very different personalities. Logan's personality has always been the same since she was very little. She was a loving, nurturing, and caring type of child. She was the motherly type who was always worried about other people and their feelings and always wanted to help others. It was amazing to see her as a little girl with such a huge heart. I was proud of her every single day. I still am.

It was only natural that Logan would graduate from high school with a desire to earn a degree in psychology. She decided to go to the local community college until she figured out exactly what concentration of psychology she wanted to focus on. She graduated from there with an Associate in Science degree and then transferred to the University of Illinois–Springfield where she graduated with her Bachelor of Arts in Psychology degree. She had a plan, she put it into action, and she accomplished her goal. She wanted to help people and get a psychology degree, and that's exactly what she did.

Shortly after graduation, Logan got hired on as a psychosocial rehabilitation services coordinator in a health care facility. There, she would have the opportunity to help people just as she always wanted, and she finished her degree that last year—while she was pregnant!

THE SHELF

The expected arrival of my very first grandson, Carter Wayne, was right around the time of Logan's graduation; so during her pregnancy, we all prayed that she'd be able to finish what she started at school and accomplish the goal she had set for herself. She didn't disappoint. Logan graduated and had Carter shortly afterward. God's timing couldn't have been more perfect, and I couldn't have been prouder of my oldest daughter—now a new wife, mother, and successful career woman.

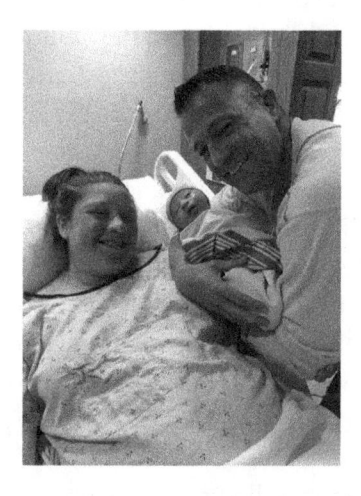

She will always be the one true blessing in my life who I know changed everything for me. When I became her dad, I became a better person despite all of my other shortcomings. Logan will always be my baby and the single greatest thing that ever happened to me.

A few years later, as Misty and I moved from Patrick Air Force base in Florida to Charleston Air Force Base in South Carolina, we decided to try and have another baby. Logan was an absolutely perfect child, and we were ready to try again to bring another one into the world. We lived in a small apartment for a while before moving onto the base; and for months, Misty and I tried to get pregnant. We didn't have much luck, so we decided to both go to the doctor to get tests done to see if we could still have kids.

Misty got checked out first, and they found that everything was fine with her. Soon after, it was my turn to get checked out. Now, I won't go into too much detail about my experience; just know that when I say I had to go get "checked out," there really wasn't much to check. They just handed me a cup and told me not to bring it back empty. Enough said?

As luck would have it, I was just fine too. But before we got my results back saying so, Misty finally got pregnant. I came home one night to a beautiful double-pink-lined pregnancy test with a little written note from Misty that simply said, "I love you," and it was the greatest feeling in the world knowing I was going to be a daddy again.

The months that followed were pretty amazing. We went through all the pregnancy stuff again, and it was fun to have Logan there too as she was somewhat old enough to realize she was going to be a big sister. She got a kick out of the whole thing and would talk about the baby often.

We were all growing more and more excited as the end of October 1998 came closer. Misty was ready to just have the baby and was trying everything she could to make it happen. Halloween came, and it seemed as though that was going to be the day it would happen. Misty was in pain and was having contractions all day long, but she stayed minimally dilated through the day and into the night, and it didn't move along as fast as I thought it would earlier in the day.

We took Logan trick-or-treating with friends and thought that maybe walking around the neighborhood would do the trick. It did; the contractions got closer and closer until we finally had to load up the car and take off for the hospital. It was between seven and eight

THE SHELF

o'clock when we got there; and once we arrived, things slowed down again.

Misty was born on Valentine's Day, and Logan was born on St. Patrick's Day, and Misty really wanted Jordan to be born on a holiday too. I'll never forget the moment when the nurse came in and told Misty that it probably wasn't going to happen. It was around eleven o'clock at night, and we were running out of time to have our Halloween baby. Of course, as much as Misty wanted it to happen on Halloween, I was perfectly okay with the baby being born the next day because that day was my birthday too.

God must've heard Misty's wishes, though, as we ended up having our Halloween baby after all. Suddenly, Misty's contractions were nonstop, she was completely dilated, and the nurse came back in and said it was time. Finally, at 11:15 that night, we welcomed Jordan Elizabeth into the world. We had our little Halloween baby, and she was perfect. I was completely in love with her from the minute I laid eyes on her. And for the second time, I had received an absolutely amazing gift from God. This time, I was blessed with "My Superstar."

Jordy was named after Michael Jordan. As a self-professed Michael Jordan superfan, it was only natural that I'd name one of my children after him. She was a perfect fit for the name as she'd end up being my little athlete and the one of my kids who'd end up being the most like me. She was a beautiful baby, full of energy and excitement. As she grew older, that never changed, and she was quite a handful most days. It was never in a bad way as all of our kids were always good, but Jordy was just always so full of energy and on the go. She was our hyper, wild, and crazy little child.

It was a different experience for Misty and me this time, mostly because we already had Logan, and the dynamic between Logan and Jordan was always so amazing. Being parents of an only child is amazing, but seeing that child welcome and nurture a younger sibling was an amazing thing for us to watch every day too. Logan was amazing with Jordy; and although that was the case, I'm sure Logan often thought Jordy was as wild and crazy as we did!

The most glaring example of Jordy's craziness comes in the form of a very embarrassing story that always seems to get told now when talking about her childhood. I've probably told the story hundreds of times as it is just such a perfect example to everyone of the type of kid she was and how interesting she made our lives on a daily basis.

I had purchased a new home for the four of us while Misty was deployed on a remote tour to South Korea for a year. The house was located off base in Summerville, and we were excited about being able to leave the base behind every day after work and live somewhere everyone you worked with wasn't all up in your business. We were fairly new to the neighborhood and hadn't really had a chance to meet our neighbors yet.

One Sunday morning, we woke up to the doorbell ringing, and I remember thinking to myself that we hadn't met anyone yet, and I didn't know who could possibly be at our door so early on a Sunday morning. I walked out of our bedroom and around the corner; and much to my surprise, I found a dining room chair and our wooden potato bin by the front door. Now you have to understand, at a very early age, our little wild one had learned to open the front door and go outside and would do so every time she could seize the opportunity. And because of that and her being so smart and full of life, Misty and I were forced to install a chain link lock on the front door. What most people do to keep people out, we had to do to keep our wild one in.

THE SHELF

Of course, on that day, she had figured out how to move a dining room chair and the potato bin just right so she could climb up, unhook the chain, and get the door open. At this point, the regular door lock was child's play for her, and it now appeared the chain link lock was no different.

I moved the chair out of the way and opened the front door. Much to my surprise, there stood Casey, one of our neighbors whom we hadn't met yet. We shook hands, and he introduced himself, and then asked me, "Does this belong to you?" As he said that, he stepped to the side and there was Jordy, sitting on her bike, looking at me with a great big smile on her face.

Now, I'm sure this doesn't seem all that funny or embarrassing to you, but you didn't get to see what I saw. Because when Casey stepped to the side, and I saw Jordy, she was sitting on her bike looking at me with a smile on her face, and she was completely naked.

Casey said he came outside and saw Jordy riding down the street on her bike with no clothes on. Obviously, he figured we probably just didn't allow it to happen, so he brought her home and let us know. It was quite the introduction to the neighborhood as you can imagine. Casey, his wife Ellen, and their kids Chelsea and Clay would end up being amazing friends and neighbors to us over the years, and we'd often get a good laugh talking about this encounter every once in a while.

Growing up, Jordy was always a lot like me. She was an athlete and played every sport you could think of and excelled at all of them. Basketball and softball were her first loves, but she also played volleyball and soccer and ran track. She loved being active and was always on the go and involved in many activities. She worked hard at everything she did, including school where she was almost always an honor roll student. Jordy was the type of girl who could put her hair in a ponytail and keep up with all the boys but could also curl her hair, put on a dress, and simply be a girl. She was my beautiful little tomboy—and always a daddy's girl. She still is to this day.

As she grew older, Jordy decided to focus on softball. She had taken hitting lessons with her coach Amanda for ten years; and every year, she got better and better. She played on traveling softball teams all over the states and was the starting second baseman on her varsity softball team all four years of high school. It was fun watching her grow up and excel in sports and in life.

She applied for college at the University of Missouri and got accepted. The day we all went up there to help her move into her dorm room was hard. Daddy's girl had become a woman, and I wasn't ready to let her go. It's not like she was that far away as she could still come home some weekends, and I could go visit her too, but it was still hard on me. I cried for hours after I got home that night. She sent me a link to the song "I Loved Her First" to remind me who I was to her, and that made the flood of tears even worse. I hadn't had this experience with Logan. I was stationed in Arizona when she started college at University of Illinois, so I wasn't there when she moved. So this college-kid-moving thing was a first for me, and it was hard.

Today, I'm so proud to say that Jordy is doing very well and has really enjoyed the full college experience. She's scheduled to finish school in three years with a bachelor's degree in marketing and sports management as the college courses she took during her senior year of high school and during the summers enable her to graduate a year early. In addition to that, she has played college softball. She has been in a sorority, she has had fun and partied and made great friends, and she did all of it while maintaining a grade point average high enough to make the dean's list. What else can you wish for as a parent? I couldn't be prouder of the woman she's become, and I'm just so blessed to be her dad.

A little while before we bought our new home and had our encounter with new neighbors, Misty had deployed on a remote tour to South Korea. Remote tours were overseas assignments where bases didn't have accommodations for families; so more often than not, we had to go alone. A year is a long time to be away from your spouse and kids, but Misty and I both had to each do it once during our careers. Fortunately for us, though, we were able to go on what they called a "midtour," which allowed us to come home for a month halfway through the yearlong tour.

Things weren't the best for Misty and me then, and we really struggled with the separation. I wasn't the best husband either as you already know, and our being thousands of miles apart didn't contribute anything positive to our already-complex relationship. But as the time got closer for Misty to come home on her midtour, things got a little better, and we were both excited about our family's being back together for a month.

When Misty got home, I couldn't have been happier to see her. I had missed her so much, and seeing her face again was an amazing feeling after all that time. Because of the issues we had prior to her deploying, I think we both just wanted to finally be happy and were always searching for the answers to make things better. Divorce was never an option for us no matter how bad things got back then. We talked a lot when she got home and definitely made up for the intimate time we lost while she was gone for six months. I include saying that because, after much discussion, we decided not to be "safe;" and if God had some master plan to bless us with a third child whom we hadn't necessarily planned for, we'd just go with it. Whatever was meant to be.

It wasn't long after that Misty found out she was pregnant. She was only home for a month, but I think it was probably our very first moment alone that did it. If I remember right, it was only a week or two after she got home that the pregnancy test showed positive.

She left for Korea a couple weeks later and returned during the summer that year in 2001. She had a nice little belly going on, and we were able to enjoy the last trimester of her pregnancy together at home with Logan and Jordy. It wasn't as we had ever envisioned; but after having two girls and having such an amazing feeling in my heart for my daughters, it didn't matter if this one was a boy or a girl—I was just ready to be a dad again for the third time.

THE SHELF

We found out we were having a girl; and this time, things wouldn't be so easy. Labor had been relatively quick for Misty when she had Logan and Jordan, so we figured the third child would be much the same or quicker. Boy were we wrong.

It wasn't until the second time we went to the hospital that it actually happened. The first time Misty had significant contractions, we thought that would be it. It was so awful to take her to the hospital and eventually be sent home because it wasn't time yet. I think it was maybe a week or two later that we went back and stayed until we had the baby. This time, Misty's labor would be more than twenty-four hours. We tried every trick imaginable. I won't freak you out with the details.

Finally, our little bundle arrived, and she was the biggest one yet. Allison Leigh cruised into the world at a healthy nine pounds and five ounces and twenty-one and one half inches—the biggest of all our kids when they were delivered. And for the third and final time, I received yet another absolutely amazing gift from God. This time, I was blessed with "My Little Bug."

Alli was just a beautiful, bouncing baby girl. There wasn't much that could phase her as she always just kind of took life in stride and was happy-go-lucky no matter what happened or what was going on around her. The dynamic between the three girls was interesting with their all having three very different personalities, but those personalities seemed to always mesh pretty well together. Logan was still caring and nurturing and motherly with her sisters, and Jordy was still wild and crazy. There was never any animosity toward Alli by the other two, but Jordy and Alli did fight a lot. Nothing major, but with their personalities being what they were, Jordy's "hyperactive" mixed with Alli's "laid back" didn't always result in sunshine and rainbows. But they all loved each other, and Alli completed our little "DeRemer 5" family, and I couldn't have been happier with how it all turned out.

Alli was involved with just about everything, much like her sisters before her. She played sports and was a cheerleader and enjoyed most of the things that she got involved in. Of course, as she grew older, she started to figure out her likes and dislikes, and sports wasn't really her thing, nor was just cheering. However, the gymnastics part of cheering was something she was very good at. She always loved to flip and do crazy stuff on the trampoline; so because she loved it and was so good at it, we put her in camps and classes to really hone her skills. She fell in love with it, so she focused on that and was able to use the skills she learned in camps and classes to turn cheerleading into something a little more interesting. She did that all the way up until she got to high school, cheering at events and games, and was even a cheerleader for Jordy's basketball team one year. It was fun to see and a perfect example of who my kids were—three girls with very distinct personalities, likes, and interests.

In addition to gymnastics, Alli always had a love for music. She didn't play an instrument but had an absolutely beautiful voice. She had participated in choir programs in junior high; but as she grew up and her voice matured, we could see just how amazing her gift really was. I think she started to realize it too. Much like what Jordy did, Alli stopped doing everything else to really focus on her music and her vocals. She spent a lot of time with her voice coach and really started to come into her own in high school. She even had an opportunity to audition for *The Voice* when they came to St. Louis.

Alli's happy-go-lucky and laid-back personality has always made her unique. As my youngest, she's still into boys and her phone and all the things that kids enjoy today in 2019. She's such an amazing young lady and more beautiful and talented then she even knows. As

I write this, she's finishing up her senior year of high school, and I'm so proud of her for the woman she's become and anxious to see what the future holds for her. She wants to go into psychology like her sister as Logan has always been a role model for her sisters and a good example for them to follow. Time will tell. Again, she's an amazing and beautiful and talented young woman and can do anything she sets her mind to. I can't wait to see exactly what that ends up being in the years to come.

Being a dad is the best thing that has ever happened to me. I've done so many things in my life, but I've not focused as much on being the best at anything as I have on being a good dad. My girls are my life, and I'd do anything in the world for them. I pray every single day that God will keep them safe and free from harm, protect them from hurt and sorrow and pain, and always take care of them no matter what they do. I'm so proud of the women my daughters have become, especially in a world today that seems to be full of entitled children who feel the world owes them something.

Misty and I did the best we could to instill good in them, to truly make them the productive members of society that they all are today. Of course, we can't take all the credit; we could only guide them. Our kids were the ones who had to be receptive to it all, make the right choices, and put in the work to be who they are today. I think they did pretty good.

I couldn't have asked for three better daughters than the ones God gave me. I love them more than they'll ever know, and I'll continue to remind them just how much I do every single day for the rest of my life. Raising them has been the greatest, most humbling, and amazing honor of my life.

CHAPTER 14

Putting Misty on the Shelf

One thing I will always be able to say for certain about Misty is that she loved me with all her heart during the first few years of our marriage. I could see it in her eyes the way she looked at me, I could hear it in her voice when she said she loved me, and I could feel it in my heart when she'd wrap her arms around me and hold me. I never doubted it for a second then. But I know now that as I seek to find the same unconditional love again in my life as an older and much wiser man, not once did I ever truly appreciate how important and rare it was to actually have it. Not after all the things I did to her during our marriage.

I was never physically abusive—that I can say with some degree of pride, if I can have any at all about who I was as a husband. However, I was verbally abusive during the beginning years of our marriage. I said things to her that I can't imagine saying to a woman today. I often called her names; I often tore her down. I did to her all the things that had been done to me.

In addition, I often found ways to leave the house to go be with friends. I also played many different sports and was gone most nights. While Misty did play sports sometimes as well, she was never going to tell me no, and was never going to put up much of a fight about the things that I wanted to go do. It wasn't because she ever feared I'd hit her or anything like that if she did, but because she truly feared she would lose me if she did, and I really took advantage of that.

I'll never forget the first time I cheated on Misty. We were still in Florida; and once the excitement of having a child had died down,

THE SHELF

I started to fall back into being the arrogant person I was prior to Misty's coming into my life. I got comfortable and stopped working on us. I was a horrible husband, and the verbal abuse continued. Misty had a voice of her own and argued back, don't get me wrong; but because I was confident she'd never leave me, I didn't care. I did what I wanted.

So during this time, we were going through some serious issues, and I had temporarily moved into an old dorm room on base to give us a cooling-down period. Leadership in our military unit absolutely loved Misty and me, so someone in our leadership chain was able to work it out so I could get a room on base for a while. It was the worst thing that anyone could have done—to not only give me free time away from my wife but also give me a place to do with what I wanted with whomever I wanted.

I don't remember the particulars of how I ended up in the position I was in, but I do know that there I was, married and in a dorm room having an affair with another woman. I cried the entire night after this woman left, knowing that I had just done something I could never take back. I knew I may not get caught; I knew Misty may never find out, but I also knew that I would never forget it. I now had to live the rest of my life knowing I was a cheater.

You see, at this point in my life, Misty was no longer a priority to me. She was only an option for me, and that's how I treated her. She deserved so much more, especially as a woman who gave her whole heart to me with the expectation that I would protect it as any man should for his wife. I didn't, and I wish I could say that I lived the rest of my life with regret and never cheated again, and we lived happily ever after, but I can't. This is a nonfiction book, and I can't just make up details as I go along to make myself look good. It was my first mistake; and unfortunately, it wouldn't be my last.

After that night with the other woman, I cried uncontrollably for hours. Then I went home. I remember the guilt and the remorse. I just wanted to rewind my life twenty-four hours and replay it all over again knowing what I knew in that moment, but I couldn't. I blew it, and that's how I felt. I was numb, but I knew I couldn't tell Misty. I knew I had to keep it a secret because, despite how much I had done to her and how high on the shelf I had put her, I knew it would destroy her. I didn't want to do that to her. I did still love her, after all.

There were other instances of infidelity; and ultimately, Misty found out about one of them, and I was forced to come clean about what had happened. I was in Korea for a year by myself, and I had succumbed to temptation. So it's not as though Misty never knew of any of it, but the initial infidelity remained a secret for more than twenty years until I started writing this book. Only then did I decide it was time to sit down and talk to her about it all. I'm not sure why I felt the need to do it, but I did.

As a Christian, I'm a firm believer that God leads us down our paths if we let Him. Free will being what it is can make you stray off His path at times; but when you have faith, and He has a plan for you, He'll get you where you're supposed to be. In this case, He laid something on my heart about Misty; it prompted a feeling so strong that I couldn't deny or ignore it. I needed to talk to her about it all and be honest. It was twenty years later, but it was just a conversation with her that I was supposed to have.

At the time, I thought maybe I needed closure. Maybe I just didn't want her to be surprised if she ever decided to buy the book and read it, although I was certain that none of it would come as a surprise to her. Maybe I still just didn't want to hurt her.

Regardless of the reason, I reached out to her, we met, and we had an amazing conversation under the night sky sitting on a park bench. I'm sure her new husband wasn't happy that she was there with me, but she came anyway. Of course, we had been divorced for almost three years. The conversation sparked old memories and was hard at times for me. When you spend eighteen years and your entire adult life with someone, you don't just forget what it felt like to love them, especially when that person is the mother of your children. And if you have any sort of heart at all, you still don't want to see them hurt.

She wasn't hurt though. In fact, we laughed quite a bit about some things and were able to put things into perspective as to why it all happened. As I said before, she wasn't really surprised by anything

THE SHELF

I had to say as her instincts were always spot-on. I think for her, it was just good for her to finally realize that her judgment was good, and she was never "crazy" all those years when she suspected some things but never knew for sure. I think there was closure for both of us once it was all said and done, and I felt very good about that—more for her than for me. Ultimately, I think God put it all on my heart to help Misty get closure, not me.

Misty is happy now and has an amazing new husband who treats her well, takes care of her, and gives her everything she was looking for in me but never got. He's an amazing father to his own children and everything a father in my shoes could ever ask for in a stepfather. There's peace of mind in knowing that, even though they live with their mom and stepfather, and I don't get to see them as often as I'd like, they're taken care of every day by someone who can be the father figure you would want them to be. Someone who you feel can be a "dad" to them as well as you can be. I don't have a problem with that, nor am I threatened by it. Some may not understand that, but I'm thankful for him. I couldn't ask for anything more for my children and for Misty.

I wish I could go back and change things with Misty some days. I wish I could go back to the days when I knew with all my heart that she loved me unconditionally, gave everything to me, trusted me, and looked at me with those eyes that said, "I will love you forever and be forever yours." I wish I could go back and truly appreciate that instead of using it and taking advantage of it to do whatever I wanted to at the time. I wish I could go back because that sort of love is exactly what I'm still searching for, and I had it all along.

As a Christian man now, though, I realize that God has a plan for all of us, and that His plan is always better than our own. I know His plan was always for things to be like this now as I sit here typing today. I try not to live my life with regret, but having been put on the shelf for so long myself makes me sorry for doing that to her for so long. And when you realize that you've carried on some of the exact traits that you didn't like happening to you while growing up, it's not a good feeling. My actions during my marriage are something I'll never be able to forget, and maybe that's good as I never want to be that man again. I've been able to forgive myself, but it's still hard to let go of the guilt knowing I was hurting someone who did nothing but love me for so long

> Husbands, love your wives as Christ loved the
> church and gave himself up for her.
>
> —Ephesians 5:25

CHAPTER 15

Faith and Fasting

My first real experience with God's power came late in December 2012 as Misty and I had reached the point when we knew our marriage was over. So much had happened in the six months prior, and it was getting increasingly difficult for us. We had spent so much time apart with both of us attending school in Alabama at different times. She went to school after I did, and then she got back home in mid-December. While nothing was really going to be figured out at Christmas time, it was inevitable that separation was near. And it's not as if the kids didn't know something was going on as I had been sleeping on the couch in the basement for weeks and tried to stay down there as much as I possibly could at the time when Misty was home.

As Christmas got closer, things just kept getting more and more difficult for me with her. I didn't really know what to do. I was just going through the motions with daily life, working out with my personal trainer and neighbor Omar, and just trying to keep my head above water through the vicious battle I was having in my heart and mind. Omar was the one who started me on my fitness journey and really was the one who taught me the ropes on weight lifting, personal training, and everything associated with both. But Omar was also a Christian man, and we'd talk often about life during or after our training sessions. And more times than not, he always had something to tell me that I never knew before. I'll always say that my journey in faith and the true beginning of my walk with God started with Omar—and calipers that determine an individual's body fat.

Now I know you're sitting there thinking, *What on earth do body fat calipers have to do with your faith and God?* Well, a lot. One day during this time around Christmas, I needed to get my body fat recalculated. Omar had done it for me when we first started training while I was preparing for my deployment to Afghanistan. That was about a year prior, so it was time to see where I was at again.

Now, you must understand Omar. He was a personal trainer with a crazy schedule, a father of three, and a husband to a woman who was also active duty air force and worked during the day. In other words, he was busy. I'd often ask Omar about doing something—again, he was my neighbor—and he would say he would, but he'd always forget about me. I never blamed him because, as I said, he was a busy man with a hectic life and schedule. So there was an expectation that when you asked Omar to do something, you'd likely have to ask him again before he'd have the chance to do it.

I was in my driveway that day. It was early in the morning on December 18th, 2012. I still remember it clearly. The sun was out, and it was unusually warm for being so close to Christmas. Omar was outside, and he came to greet me in the middle of the street as always for our handshake and "bro hug" like we did every time we saw each other. I told him I wanted to get my body fat done again; and of course, he never said when he'd do it, he just said it wasn't a problem, and he would get to the house sometime, and we'd get it done—just like he always said.

We talked a little more, and then went about our day with me walking away knowing full well I would have to remind him again in a day or two if I really wanted to make sure I got it done. It was always that way with him, so I grew to understand that and timed my requests accordingly.

Oddly enough, the doorbell rang about thirty minutes later. I was in the kitchen drinking coffee that I had gotten from the gas station earlier that morning. As I made my way around the corner to the doorway, I noticed Omar standing there, with body fat caliper kit in hand. I remember thinking to myself jokingly that something must be wrong with him because he never just showed up when I needed something after asking him only once. I opened the door and proceeded to tell him that he didn't have to do it right then; but he had his stuff and said he was ready, so he did.

Once we were done, we stood there talking for a little while. We had previously talked enough for him to know something was visibly wrong with me, and he inquired about it. Omar was a former competitive bodybuilder and an African American born and raised in Panama. He had every bit of the accent too. I only mention these things to give you the visual of what I was staring at. A mountain of a man with a heart of gold—a Christian man, a man who would proceed to tell me something I had never heard before and something that would force me to trust like I had never trusted before in my life.

I told him how I was feeling about my marriage and what I was going through. He quoted scripture and consoled me. And then, after my going on and on about how I was feeling about things, he exclaimed loudly in his thick accent, "I know what we must do. We must fast!"

I knew what fasting was, but not so much in biblical terms. That's what I told Omar at the time. He then proceeded to tell me more about it and how it was a way for you to put full faith and trust in God. Obviously, the body requires food for sustenance; so during a fast, you truly had to put full faith and trust in God and focus with all your heart and mind on Him to get through it. It also had to be done with humility—with sincerity and good intentions—and as you already know, humility and I didn't necessarily get along all that well for most of my life.

But here I was, standing in my kitchen about to hit rock bottom, and I was willing to do whatever it took to take the pain away. It only took minutes of Omar's talking about it to have me convinced it was something I needed to do, and I was convinced that this meeting was happening for a reason that day.

I threw my almost-full cup of coffee into the sink and said, "Let's do it." I remember turning around to look at the clock on the microwave to see it was ten o'clock in the morning. I'm not sure why I so easily decided that this was the right thing to do as I had never done it before, and the thought of not eating wasn't necessarily a good thing in my mind. But in that moment, I didn't question what

Omar was saying; I just took a giant leap of faith and trusted what he was saying and trusted that God would provide as Omar said he would.

This is going to be the start of my fast, I thought, and nothing or no one was going to stop me from doing it and doing it right.

When Omar left, I picked up my phone and started researching. I scoured web site after web site, learning about fasting and everything that was involved with fasting and why people do it. There were sites on fasting in general, sites about absolute fasting, and sites about why people fast. There were one-day fasts, three-day fasts, weeklong fasts, and twenty-eight-day fasts. My head was spinning. I had absolutely no idea what kind of fast to do and for how long I was supposed to do it. I needed to figure it out. Of course, that was my first mistake, thinking that it was something I had to figure out. It wasn't. God already had His plan in place and knew how long I was to do it, and it wasn't long until he finally let me know.

It was Christmastime, of course, so I had plenty of shopping to do for the kids to keep my mind occupied that day. After clearing my head of all the things I had just read about fasting, I decided to go to the mall to do some Christmas shopping. I generally had a routine anytime I went to the mall: park in the food court parking lot, go in the side door closest to where Starbucks was located, and get coffee to drink while I was walking through the mall. It was habit, so that's exactly what I did. Of course, once I walked in, I realized that I had just started a fast and there wasn't going to be any coffee for me that day. In that moment, I just shook my head and realized that this was going to be much harder than I thought.

Shortly after that, I found clarity in my fasting dilemma. I mention Starbucks because it was right when I walked past Starbucks and avoided getting that coffee that I realized how long I was to do my fast. God was clearly speaking to me in that moment. My mind was flooded with overwhelming thoughts of a seven-day fast. I couldn't get it out of my mind. It was almost as if there were neon signs all around me that said, "Seven days," and little voices inside my head screaming, *Seven days!* That's the only way I can think of to describe the overwhelming feeling I suddenly had about fasting for seven days. So in keeping with everything I had read about God's being the one to dictate the timing of it all, a seven-day fast it was.

All day long, I hadn't eaten a thing and didn't drink an ounce of anything either, to include water. I was miserable. There were so many times during the day, after finding that clarity, that I thought there was no way I could ever go a week without eating. Later that night, I lay in bed and did some more research on fasting and would find that what I was doing was called an absolute fast (no food and no water) and discovered that it was dangerous to do an absolute fast if you were new to fasting and hadn't prepared your body for it. Going that long without water, they said, was dangerous for new fasters; and unless you truly felt that God was calling you to do an absolute fast, you shouldn't do it. At that time, I was so unsure of what type of fast I was supposed to do that I didn't feel compelled to do the absolute fast. So having found information that warned me about not having water, I took that as a sign—God was leading me toward a water-only fast.

I chronicled my fast in the "notes" section of my phone. I'm not sure that it's something most fasters do, but I felt compelled to do it. This book is probably why. I still have it in my notes to this day, more than six years later. Here are my exact notes (without edit) from day one after my conversation with Omar, with explanations as needed:

> Fasting Start
> Day 1—18 Dec 12, 1000
> 172 lbs.
> Started an absolute fast. No food, no water for 7 days until Xmas morning. Update: Decided to do 24-hr no food, no water…then a full week of water-only fasting (no food) due to safety/health reasons

I had decided to start my "log" of the fast in the morning right after talking to Omar. The update you see came later that night after it became very clear what I was meant to do.

Day 2—19 Dec
168.5 lbs.
Hunger pangs started. Seemed like every TV commercial had to do w food. Doing well. Was glad to have water at 1000 though. Very glad. Still did a great shoulder workout even w no food. God's strength was w me and I continued to ask for it. No one has noticed I haven't eaten anything for almost two full days, thank goodness. I can focus on me and my relationship w God and not questions abt what I'm doing and why. They wouldn't understand and would likely think I'm being stupid.

I waited the full twenty-four hours before I had water. So even though I wanted water in the worst way after going the first day without it, I waited until ten in the morning the second day to have any.

Day 3—20 Dec
168 lbs.
Wasn't expecting much weight loss today since I started drinking water yesterday. The weird dreams started last night already. Felt tested today…went to the store to get stuff for Xmas dinner. Going to Misty's SCC Xmas lunch today too. That will be a challenge for sure not to eat… and probably the first time I will have to come up w a reason why not…wasn't tempted to eat, but was hungry. Misty just thought I wouldn't eat because it was all junk food, so no worries on really having to explain anything. Still doing well…hungry, but manageable. Think the detox has started. I'm starting to feel the nausea and pain in my stomach like things are starting to break up in there.

THE SHELF

During my research on fasting, I read a lot about what some people may experience during a fast. Having strange dreams was one of the things I read about; and as you see in the log for this day, I had started having some. "SCC" was the name of the flight Misty worked in the air force. They were having their section Christmas party at a bar with plenty of fried junk food. When I mentioned that I was "tempted to eat," that was the update after we returned home from that party. Looking back now, I'm not even sure why I chose to go with her. The "detox" is exactly what you think it is. I'm sure I don't need to go into any graphic details.

> Day 4—21 Dec
> 168 lbs.
> Detox def seems to have started. For not having eaten any food for three days, some odd stuff came out of me this morning. Not much though. Nausea set in for most of the day. Not horrible though. Lightheadedness continues as do the headaches. Started to feel a little of the flu symptoms kicking in too. Misty got pizza for dinner. That was tough. Alli made brownies too and the whole house smelled like them. Ugh. I was real hungry today and tempted. Held strong though. Day 5 here I come.

As I said, I don't think I need to go into detail about the detox. Nausea, light-headedness, and headaches were things I read that could happen during a fast, and I certainly felt all of it. The flu-like symptoms were also something I read about, so I wasn't concerned with that. Watching my kids and wife eat pizza after not eating for four days was one of the most difficult things ever. If ever there was a true definition of "mouthwatering," I was experiencing it that night. The brownies just made it worse. I just kept thinking, *Let me just go to bed and warp to tomorrow and away from all this!* Of course, it was Christmastime, and with what I knew would soon become my reality, I was going to stay right where I was and continue to spend as much time with my children as I could no matter how horrible I was feeling.

> Day 5—Dec 22
> 167.5 lbs
> No real weight loss the past couple days. Back pain is continuing, along with feeling like I have a cold or the flu. Not bad, but I can feel it. Detox continues. Funky stuff came out of me this morning. Yuck. Getting more winded and tired. Worked the Illinois game tonight. That was tough. I'm so hungry and handling all that food was hard. My back is really starting to hurt too. Really starting to get hard. Putting my faith in God to help me through it.

Back pain was another thing I had read could happen during a fast. With my already-existing back problems, this fast was just exacerbating the problem. I was starting to feel the effects of no food on my energy level; and as a personal trainer also certified in fitness nutrition, I now fully understand what my body was craving during this time. I had no fuel. My daughter played on a select softball team at the time, and we would often volunteer to work a food stand at the Edward Jones Dome during basketball games, hockey games, football games, and concerts to raise money. Of course, as luck would have it, we had previously volunteered to work a food-and-drink stand right smack dab in the middle of my fast. God surely knew what He was doing long before I did about this fast. Every test imaginable seemed to be present during those long seven days.

> Day 6—Dec 23
> 165.5 lbs
> Not feeling too bad today. Hunger isn't bad and nausea is minimal, if any. Hungry a little, but no trouble with temptation. No detox to speak of yet. Hungry at night. Misty finally asked when it

> was I ate last. Was able to play it off. She thinks I'm dieting, so I haven't had to answer many questions. Misty and Alli made sugar cookies. That was tough to resist. Alli and Misty eating chips while we played pool was difficult, but I resisted temptation. Day 6 is over. One day left. Finding strength and about to finish something I never thought I could do.

Nothing really to talk about after this day. As you can see, my body was starting to get used to things and feeding off whatever it could for energy. Six days without having to answer questions was good; although as I said, I was able to play it off pretty good with Misty when she asked that day. The sugar cookie thing is significant because they're my favorite. That was probably the hardest thing of all to turn away from, especially when your child has made them, knows they're your favorite, and proceeds to find you to give you one to eat. I made it work so I didn't hurt her feelings though, although I would have given it all up at that point if I knew that would've ever been the case. I think God would have understood.

> Day 7—Dec 24
> 165 lbs.
> No detox. Hungry, but manageable. Worried about tomorrow. Don't want to undo all the good I've done. Have to eat plenty of vegetables before dinner I guess.

The last day wasn't all that hard, likely because there was light at the end of the tunnel toward food, and the excitement of Christmas with the kids was in the air. I had read about easing back into your diet once a fast was complete, so that's what I was worried about that day. With all the good food that was coming on Christmas and my tendency to gorge myself all day long, I was concerned that my hunger would take over my brain.

I didn't write any notes on Christmas morning. Misty always made deviled eggs and put out a vegetable tray around ten o'clock in the morning on Christmas for all of us to munch on before dinner in the early afternoon. It ended up working out perfectly as my seven-day fast was complete at ten o'clock; and by the time the kids had torn into all their presents, and we made our way back upstairs to start preparations for dinner, it was ten o'clock, and I could eat again. And that was the end of that. I made it. (If you're curious, the very first thing I ate was an apple that was in a fruit basket on our bar. We normally kept the basket full of apples and oranges for the kids. It was the best apple I ever ate.)

It's hard to put into words the feeling I had during and after that time. The range of emotions you go through when fasting that long for the first time is vast. I laughed, I cried, I got angry, and got frustrated. I prayed nonstop that I could make it because I felt I was being led to do it and didn't want to fail. While my faith was still so brand-new, I knew enough to know that I didn't want to fail God and disappoint Him and what I felt He was calling me to do. Of course, I know now that God would never have been disappointed in me, but that fast instilled something in me that I hadn't had before, and I will never forget the experience or how it came about. It led to so much more that I never saw coming as is the case with just about everything God does for those who truly believe in Him.

I can sum up the whole experience for you by saying this: Earlier in this chapter, I mentioned that I started my fast on the morning of December 18th, then I mentioned that I discovered later the same afternoon that God's plan for me was to do a seven-day fast. It wasn't until that night that I put it all together. Some of you may have already done so yourself by now. There was a reason why Omar did my fat body measurements that day. There was a reason why I didn't ask him a day earlier and why he didn't show up a day later. My fast was supposed to start on that day and end seven days later. It was God's plan. That's how He wanted it to happen to strengthen my faith, to make me a believer, because seven days later was December 25th—seven days later was Christmas.

THE SHELF

That was my first true experience with the power of God and Jesus Christ and truly feeling like God had His hands on my life. And after experiencing this, I didn't just want God in my life, I needed him in it.

> And if you faithfully obey the voice of the Lord your God, being careful to do all his commandments that I command you today, the Lord your God will set you high above all the nations of the earth. And all these blessings shall come upon you and overtake you, if you obey the voice of the Lord your God.
>
> —Deuteronomy 28:1–2

CHAPTER 16

Divorce and Bodybuilding

When I first left Misty on January 1st, 2013, it was extremely hard on me. Things had just continued to get worse over eighteen years, and we grew further and further apart as each year passed. Logan, Jordan, and Allison were starting to get older and starting to understand more and finally got to the age where we felt they'd understand why we made the choice to go through with a divorce. It wasn't easy, but it was right—for their sake and ours.

It was the first time in my adult life that I was alone and the first time being separated from my children. At first, I spent hours wanting to just go home. I was missing my kids and was just wishing everything could go back to the way it was. But knowing that wasn't healthy for me or the right thing to do, I needed to do something to focus my mind on something else, so I turned to weight lifting.

I dove headfirst into the whole thing. I researched weight training routines, joined sites, learned about nutrition, and did as much as I could to focus on something other than the negatives in my life at the time. During that journey, my body really started transforming. People were noticing. I would often get asked what I was doing or told that I should think about becoming a personal trainer. Of course, that was something I just never thought I'd do at the time.

I ended up getting my first three of four certifications in personal training, fitness nutrition, and exercise therapy later that summer in 2013. However, I didn't begin to go out and seek clients as I wanted to truly make sure I knew what I was doing and have the credibility to teach people before I tried to build a client base. So I started experimenting with the nutrition part on myself to see how macronutrients and diet and weight lifting really worked. I wanted to see how I could change my own body by using the tools and resources and information provided to me in my training and education. I was going to be my own experiment.

What happened after that was a transformation like I could never have imagined. I was stunned; people in the gym were stunned. On almost a daily basis, people would stop and ask me what I was doing and ask if I could help them transform like I had. It was crazy for a while. It was hard for me to believe what was happening and how much I was changing.

Around that time, Omar mentioned that I should compete in a bodybuilding competition in late June of 2013. I immediately discounted the thought of ever doing something like that and thought he was crazy. I was, after all, thirty-eight years old and would be competing against kids who were half my age. I just knew it wasn't in the cards for me—or so I thought at the time.

I ended up doing that competition in June. I placed fifth, capturing the last of the five trophies they awarded that day—a top five finish in my first competition. I was on cloud nine. It was so much work and discipline and sacrifice. It was something I never thought I'd ever do, but it was worth it. In that moment, I had checked a box and accomplished something I thought was impossible.

Ultimately, natural bodybuilding changed my life. The people I met in the natural bodybuilding world were amazing, and the friends I made were amazing; it was an amazing fraternity to be a part of. We all shared the same goals and understood the same struggles. We all worked as hard as we possibly could, and sometimes we didn't always get the results we were shooting for. Regardless, we all shared a common bond that most will never understand. It was a part of my life that I'll never forget and will be forever thankful for.

I ended up competing in seventeen shows over three years, winning five times and earning four "best poser" awards and three pro cards. I also competed in my first pro show on my fortieth birthday, placing third. The perfect way to welcome the forties, don't you think?

Or do you not know that your body is a temple of the Holy Spirit within you, whom you have from God? You are not your own, for you were bought with a price. So glorify God in your body.

—1 Corinthians 6:19–20

CHAPTER 17

Her

Beautiful. Blond. Sexy. Talented. Smart. Funny.

Those words don't even begin to describe the woman who completely changed my world and how I viewed every other woman in it. To me, Misti was the perfect woman—the one who had everything I had been searching for my entire life. (Note: this is the point where you note the different spelling of the name "Misti." This Misti is a different person than the Misty who is now my ex-wife. Don't get confused. Mist(y) with a Y—ex-wife. Mist(i) with an I—girlfriend.)

Misti and I lived on the same street in our neighborhood. Prior to leaving my wife, I would often see Misti, her husband, and her kids as they'd pass by our house or be outside of theirs. I didn't really know her all that well at the time but had met her at a neighborhood party once and remember being absolutely floored by how stunning she was. To me, she was one of those women you just don't forget about.

She and I worked out in the same gym on base and had the same circle of friends. It was at this point that we started to get to know each other more. I worked out with my personal trainer (who would eventually become hers), and you could always find Misti in the gym on a treadmill. She was an avid runner, running for miles and miles every single day. And we seemed to always be in the gym at the same time.

As we became friends, we talked a lot more. According to her, she was very unhappy in her own marriage and had fallen out of love with her husband. And since I had already left my wife at the time and was waiting for my own divorce to be final, Misti and I related on many levels when it came to how we felt, what we were going through, and what we wanted out of life and love.

We were friends for a long time. The intimate nature of our conversations and the very private details we shared with each other about our marriages started to change things. A great bond was slowly forming between us. I recognized it and tried to tread lightly as time went on as she was just a beautiful and amazing woman. I had to tread lightly. I think she tried too. It wasn't that I didn't find her attractive—I did. Again, she was a beautiful and amazing woman.

My reservation at first was because, despite her desires to end her marriage, she was still married. And I was trying to live a Christlike life and protect my path, knowing that infidelity was wrong in the eyes of God. At the time, I didn't even know if she would even get a divorce, no matter what she said to me about her relationship. I just wanted to do the right thing by God; and despite how difficult it was to not pursue things further, I just couldn't—we couldn't. And once the realization came that we couldn't take the relationship further, we were able to just be friends, and everything was good.

As time went by, the friendship began to mature and grow more. We continued to talk about life and love. I had already left my wife, and my divorce was almost final. Misti and I had so much in common and had so many mutual feelings to share about what we wanted out of life—and in a partner. Our past experiences had made us both who we were at the time; and the more we talked without the pressure of being in a relationship ourselves, the more our emotional connection started to develop. It was undeniable. But she still wasn't divorced, was still living at home with her husband, and at that point had no plans to get a divorce that I knew of. So it started to get hard for me—very hard. And little did I know that this would only be the beginning of the hardships that were to come for me.

During this time, I found out Misti was preparing to run the LA Marathon in March 2013. It was interesting to hear about her preparation and the unbelievable number of miles she had to log before even getting to the marathon itself. We talked daily as she'd always be in the gym running on the treadmill when I'd arrive at the gym to work out after work. She was always there, always smiling, always laughing, always looking at me like no one had ever looked at me before. At times, I'd daydream about her and the "what ifs," but tried to be realistic about where we were at in our lives at the time. Despite that, I just couldn't help feeling like maybe someone was starting to love me with that unconditional type of love I had been searching for again.

At this point, you can probably guess what happened next. Our friendship grew into a best friendship, and I could feel more and more things changing in me as time went on. I still wasn't where I needed to be to move forward with her, but something significant was happening. I still had no idea what it was, but more and more often during my quiet times, my mornings alone, and my weekends lying on my couch, I would think of her.

We messaged each other on Facebook on occasion; and one day while at work, she messaged me from California and talked a little about how she felt about running the marathon. She discreetly mentioned that there was a way people could track her status online as she ran the marathon; and of course, I asked for the information in case I wanted to follow her and see how she was doing. As it turned out, that's exactly what I did. And not only did I track her every move that day as I sat in my living room, I posted about it and kept all our friends up to date who weren't tracking her themselves. I'm not sure why I got so excited about it, but I did. I felt good about it; it felt good to support her doing something I'd watched her train and work so hard for months for. I was so proud of her; and as I posted updates, I found myself more and more just wanting to be there with her.

In the days that followed once she got home, Misti expressed her feelings about how my posts made her feel. She was happy; she said she felt supported and important and wanted. Our feelings were getting stronger toward each other, and our friendship continued to grow even stronger after she returned home from California.

As I said in the last chapter, I started competing in natural bodybuilding in June of 2013. My first show was on June 29th, and Misti was there. It was a brand-new experience for me with the spray tan and the board shorts and showing off my new body to the hundreds of people watching. It ended up being very awkward too as my ex-wife Misty, who was seeking reconciliation at this point, was also there watching along with my children and my best friend Michael.

It was interesting to say the least. I had no interest in getting back together with my ex-wife, nor was I really thinking about seriously starting a relationship with Misti. But there I was, about to be completely vulnerable on stage, and in the audience sat my ex-wife and an amazing woman whom I was starting to develop feelings for and who had become my best friend.

I think Misty knew after the show that our marriage was over for good. I didn't pay much attention to her during and after the show, so I think that was finally it for her. Misti came to support me, said goodbye after the show was over, and went on her way. She was proud of me; I could see that in her eyes. Her being there meant the world to me as I think we both truly wanted more than we were willing to give at that time. I'm not sure either of us knew how to even move forward with it. But as much as I kept trying to fight what I was feeling, my feelings for her were getting stronger and stronger. I just knew I couldn't do anything about it.

Coming off the high of the top five finish the night before, I got a message from a promoter named Steven the following morning, congratulating me and inviting me to do his show a month later. I was excited about the fact that a promoter had reached out to me to do it. I mean, at this point, who was I in the natural bodybuilding world? I was a nobody; no one knew me, I was brand-new, and this guy really had no reason to reach out to me, did he? (He and I would end up becoming good friends and still are to this day). Regardless, I sat on the floor in my living room reading his message and responded with "send me the information!" And not more than thirty minutes later, I was registered for my second bodybuilding competition. I was truly excited about it too. This was really where my bodybuilding journey really began.

That next competition was on August 2nd, 2013; and because I was already in competition shape, there wasn't much more for me to do other than stay on my diet and keep working out as I had been to prepare for the previous competition. I ended up telling Misti about it, of course; and as you can probably guess, she was there in the audience during that show too. We had some ups and down between shows as I think we were both just trying to figure out what was going on with us, so I didn't know if she'd be there, but she was. It wasn't until I was on stage and heard her voice that I knew for sure that she was; and in that moment, I felt safe. I felt comfortable; I felt loved; it felt good to have someone be so supportive, so loving, and so willing to do whatever it took to show that to me. As I said, things were changing inside of me; and after that, it started to get to the point where I just couldn't deny it any longer.

I ended up winning that show and earning the "best poser" award. I was completely shocked and happy and excited, and I experienced just about every emotion someone can feel when they accomplish something they never in their life thought was possible. Here I was, a thirty-eight-year-old man competing against twenty-year-old kids, and I had just won. It was amazing.

THE SHELF

After the show, I went to the after party they threw at a bowling alley nearby. I invited Misti to go with my trainer and me, and she did. We sat there for a while, and I ate an obscene amount of food and talked to people as I just took in everything that had just happened to me. Suddenly, I was somebody. Everyone was asking what show was next and where would I go. Yet in that moment, the only thing I could think about was hearing that voice on stage and wondering what was next in another important part of my life that wasn't bodybuilding.

As the party was winding down, Misti had to leave. I told my trainer that I'd be right back, and I walked her out to her car as any gentleman should in that situation. I opened her car door as I always did, and she sat down in the seat. We talked for a second, and then as I said goodbye, I leaned in and kissed her. It was nothing major as far as kisses go, but it felt good. It was something we both had wanted for a long time.

Misti and I got close after that. She would visit me at my house, and we'd talk, but things still never got to the point where I felt a true relationship had begun. She'd visit, leave notes in my mailbox, send me messages letting me know she was thinking about me, and things like that. They were all things that I had wanted for so long in my marriage that I wasn't getting because during my marriage, I felt like I was the one who had been trying and getting nothing in return. And once you get to the point where you're saying, "Why bother?"—you just don't bother anymore. Not that I blame Misty for that during our marriage, after being the horrible husband I was. But feeling what I was starting to feel with Misti was amazing. It was confusing for me at the time, but still amazing. It didn't feel like the love I had always known; this was different.

At this point, I realized that bodybuilding was something I was meant to do. With a classic men's physique look, it was only natural for me to compete in the new men's physique class. The class that was generally regarded as the one for guys who have a great smile and a good set of abs. None of us were huge like most people think of when they hear the word "bodybuilder." We were the pretty boys; we were more fitness model than powerlifter. And I loved it; I loved how I

THE SHELF

felt, I loved what was happening, and I loved finally having a goal to shoot for. Preparing for the "next show" became a huge part of who I was over the next few years. Finishing one show and looking for the next was one of the most exhilarating feelings I've ever had in my life as most competitors can likely attest to as well. So after winning my second show, I started looking for the next one and found another show to do a month later, this time in Kansas City.

The Kansas City Classic show was in Overland Park, Kansas, about four hours away from where I lived in Southern Illinois. As she had done for my two previous competitions, Misti made plans to be there and was going to make the road trip with a girlfriend, Jenn, who happened to be a mutual friend of ours. Because Jenn was coming along also, I didn't have an issue with allowing them to both stay with me in the hotel as they could sleep together in the same bed while I slept in the other bed. I got a room with two beds, and it would work out fine. And I would have some support and not be alone. In my mind, this arrangement and having a third person there would take away the awkwardness for Misti and I being there together. It would also allow us to just enjoy the experience together as best friends without temptation clouding our judgment and taking away from that experience.

I made it to Kansas City early as I had taken leave from my air force job to get there a day early. This gave my body time to acclimate and relax prior to registration, polygraph, tans, meetings, and all the precompetition things we had to do. Misti and Jenn couldn't leave until after work that day, so I got to Kansas City a few hours before they would even be able to leave Illinois.

As the hour approached when they were supposed to leave and head my way, I got a text from Misti saying she wasn't going to be able to make it. Of course, that didn't make any sense after how excited she had been all week about coming and all the things we had talked about doing after the show. But despite the thoughts I had about that, I couldn't help but immediately feel disappointment; my heart sank. It was another one of those moments when I felt something happening but didn't quite know what it was. All I knew in that moment was that I wanted her there; and suddenly, she wasn't going to be.

As it turned out, the next text I got was a photo of Misti and Jenn in the car with a message that said, "Just kidding. We are on our way!" And as quickly as my heart had sunk, it immediately felt full, and I felt extremely happy and excited. At this point, it wasn't really because of anything other than just feeling good about people caring enough about me to support me, something I was never used to. And in this case, here was a woman who loved me enough to drive four hours to spend a weekend with me to support me in my goals and the things that were important to me. That was new, and *that* felt good.

Misti and Jenn arrived later that night, and it was exciting to have them there to share the experience with. At that time, neither of them had competed themselves, and they were just taking it all in, just as I had been in the previous two shows. We sat in the audience and watched other classes go before me and just enjoyed each other and the experience as time went on. It was finally my time to go on stage, and I was as confident and excited as ever to be there. Misti was guiding me, yelling for me, and doing the normal Misti things she had done in the previous shows. She had become my comfort zone without me even realizing it. She made all this okay for me.

I did well; and after I got off stage, Misti said she thought I had won. She always did well with predicting where I'd place—and no, she didn't blow smoke by saying "I think you won" every time. However, in this case, she did feel that I had. I felt confident and comfortable at this point and just remember feeling good about the feedback she gave me. Of course, she was supposed to say that, wasn't she? She always had a way to say just the right things—and with a sincerity I never questioned. We had grown to have such an amazing bond up to that point, and I knew she loved me—and that felt good to know, despite our circumstances.

Generally, after you go on stage for what they call "prejudging"—the part of the competition where judges do comparisons and initial competitor scoring—there are a few hours before the night show begins where competitors do individual posing routines and find out the winners and receive awards. After prejudging, most competitors just go back to their hotel rooms and relax because posing during prejudging can be exhausting, especially if you've been depleted on carbohydrates and have limited your water intake prior to going on stage. So going back to the hotel room was exactly what we did, and that's where my relationship with Misti changed, as did my life and future moving forward.

Misti had brought a portable speaker with her so we could listen to music while in the hotel room. We were there relaxing and talking and music was playing. There was nothing special about what was going on, nor was there any music theme happening that I can remember. I just remember feeling confident about how I had done and was ready to go do my presentation walk and finish what I had set out to do. Misti was lying on one of the beds and her friend was walking around the room doing something. I had just lain down in my own bed to rest, and that's when it happened.

I've always loved the country band Thompson Square. As anyone who knows me would tell you, I'm a music guy. I've always loved music that has a message, and country music more than most has been the type of music that's gotten me through many things over the years.

As I lay there in this hotel room bed, the song "That's So Me and You" came on, and I immediately felt tears coming on. I didn't know why, and I didn't know what to do. I didn't know what was happening. All I knew at that point was that I was completely overcome with emotion and about to unleash tears and cry in a room with two women. Well my alpha male self was not going to allow that to happen. So I did what any person would do who was trying to hide tears from people—I covered up my face with a two-foot pillow and went into the bathroom with it over my face. So much for discretion.

I can still see what my face looked like through that hotel bathroom mirror. Red bloodshot eyes and uncontrollable tears. I wasn't upset in a way that produced incoherent babbling or hyperventilating, but tears did flow, and they were very real ones. I remember staring at the shiny chrome faucet; and as I looked up to stare myself in the face, I said out loud to myself, "What is happening?" And it was in that moment that I finally realized I had fallen in love with Misti.

I walked out of the bathroom to Misti's puzzled look and scrunched-up eyebrows and immediate question: "What's wrong?" Of course, my discretion (or lack thereof) was a complete and total failure. Honestly, I don't remember exactly how I deflected her question, but I was able to do that successfully enough to avoid answering it as we all then took naps and waited for the night show. I didn't sleep much as my mind was racing, and my brain just wouldn't turn off. I had fallen in love with a married woman—a woman I couldn't have, a woman I couldn't be with, but also a woman who also loved me as much as I had just realized I loved her.

This spells trouble, I thought to myself, but it didn't stop how we felt, nor did it keep a relationship from forming shortly afterward. It put me on a completely different course than I had ever imagined. It changed everything, and I had no idea about the roller-coaster ride I was about to be on in the three years that followed with her.

> And above all these is love, which binds
> everything together in perfect harmony.
>
> —Colossians 3:14

CHAPTER 18

Moving Mountains

In August 2013, my divorce became final, and things changed quite a bit for me. The summer with Misti and competing had been amazing so far; although at this point, we hadn't gone to Kansas City yet, and I still hadn't realized I was falling in love with her. I had lived on my own for eight months and was preparing for retirement about this time. I had become a personal trainer and was doing that part-time also, training a few clients here and there and trying to build an online diet program and nutrition business at the same time. Life was good.

As a personal trainer, I often visited one of my clients in her home, using what equipment and furniture she had available to give her the best workout possible. She was retired, and her husband was a retired air force chief master sergeant, so we always had different subjects to talk about, from life in general to military politics and all that came with it. They were good friends and always seemed to have an interest in me, my career, and what I would end up doing in the future after I retired from the military.

They had a screenhouse attached to their kitchen that oversaw a lake in their backyard. Chief would, more times than not, be sitting in a chair out there doing something when we'd finish training, and I'd stand in the doorway and chat with him for a little while before I left. He always had such good insight about the military and life, and I was always open to the things he had to say. He had lived through many of the things I had gone through in the air force already, so I always looked forward to our conversations and how his perspective on things could sometimes change or alter my own.

One day, we got into a conversation about my preparing for retirement and what my plans were going to be. Of course, as a bodybuilder and personal trainer, I thought at the time that training people was going to be what I'd do full-time. However, I've always been one to never close any doors and to always have my eyes and ears open to whatever plans God has for me. Chief asked me why I wouldn't just stay in the air force and try to make chief myself.

In the air force, chief master sergeant is the highest enlisted rank you can achieve, and you have thirty years to do it before reaching high year tenure and being forced to retire. At this point, I was a senior master sergeant—the rank just below chief—and had just over twenty years in the air force. I had plenty of time, experience, and accomplishments to become a chief for sure.

I responded by telling the chief that I just knew it was my time. I'm not sure I believed that at the time, but it was how I felt in that moment. Chief then responded by asking me, "Is there anything that would happen to make you change your mind and stay in the air force?"

I thought about it for a second and told him, "Well, Chief, if a job to Luke Air Force Base in Arizona suddenly became available, I might have to just reconsider. But that's the only way I would, and that will never happen." I said it as a joke, knowing full well that this job and location had eluded me for years and would just never become available for me at this point in my career. I had become very content and at peace with my decision to retire and was sure that that's what was going to happen.

THE SHELF

A day or two later, I was in my office having a conversation with a coworker named Maja about retiring. Maja didn't want me to go as she and I got along amazingly while not necessarily getting along or fitting in with everyone else in the office. It was a headquarters job full of headquarter politics and drama, most of which we just tried to stay out of. Regardless, Maja didn't want me to leave and would always make a joke about not letting me go.

During the course of the conversation, I was taken aback by the fact that she asked me the same exact question that the chief had asked me a day or two prior. And with my response to the chief still fresh in my mind, I told Maja the same thing I told the chief. She asked, "Why Arizona?" just like chief did, and I responded the same way—that all I had ever heard were good things from people who either grew up there or were stationed there, and that I loved sun and palm trees!

The conversation with Maja faded, and I didn't think much of either of those conversations after the fact. However, they both may have subconsciously prompted me to do something I may not have otherwise done: get on the computer and look at the air force assignments portal to see what special duty assignments were out there to apply for.

My divorce was officially final a few days later in August as I said, and I remember coming back from the courthouse knowing it was done and thinking about how different my life was going to be, being single again after eighteen years of marriage. Of course, it never really was all that different as Misti was in my life at this time, and my feelings had started for her (remember, our relationship had already kind of started at this point, but I didn't realize I was actually in love with her until Kansas City about a month later). But as I had those thoughts of being newly single in the technical sense, I remember thinking about the conversations I had with the chief and with Maja and just being curious.

As I sat there, I was reminded by the vast amount of deployment training I had piling up on my desk that I was already selected to go on a deployment to Africa for six months starting in October. Immediately, I discounted anything else in my mind that didn't include that and retirement. My plans were to deploy, return from deployment, and then retire—that's it. My kids were in Illinois where I was stationed, I knew people to build a good personal training client base, and I had been there for five years already. It was what was meant to be; that's what I was supposed to do. That was my plan—my plan.

With my journey as a Christian really starting after I left my wife in January 2013, I felt like I was on a good path, especially after completing my fast. And after a night of total and complete misery shortly after that, thinking about Misty and my kids, I decided to just let go and let God take control of my life. I had hit rock bottom soon after I left her and had no idea what to do anymore. I got tired of crying, tired of fighting for something that wasn't working, and tired of hurting. So I let go.

I'll never forget that day, lying in bed, staring up at the ceiling, and with tears in my eyes saying, "I give it all to you now, God. I can't do this by myself anymore." And that's when everything started to change—I started to change. Things started to get easier. I felt better about myself. I got over my wife and moved on. I still had some rough times but finally let go, and God surely took over.

Between January and that day in my office in August, there were so many signs that God was in my life—from an unexpected check arriving in the mail hours after I had prayed to Him about being worried about not being able to pay my bills to reuniting with old friends who reached out after twenty years who were struggling from the same heartaches I had just gotten over myself. He used me for sure and helped me too. And every time something like that happened, it renewed my faith in Him and helped me grow stronger and stronger as a Christian every single day. It's something I am so grateful and thankful for every day now.

So, returning to August and sitting there in my office after coming back from the courthouse after my divorce was final, the thoughts about checking for new jobs and assignments sparked my curiosity. Misty was also in the air force at the time; and when they had moved us throughout our careers, they couldn't do so until they found jobs for both of us at any given location (called the

THE SHELF

Joint Spouse Program for those military-married-to-military couples). This prevented me from getting many jobs I wanted over the course of twenty years, Luke Air Force Base being one of them. And now that my divorce was final, this was the first time in my twenty-year career where I could look for an assignment without having to worry about that.

Even though I was scheduled to deploy and was preparing for retirement, I guess there was just something inside of me that was curious. I'd find out later that something was God—just up there tugging on the strings of my life to get me where He wanted. Because my life from this point forward was never going to be about my plan; it was going to be about His.

I had two computers on my desk, a laptop I used that was on a commercial network for us to access websites for social media that the government network wouldn't allow and my normal desktop on the government network I used for other military-related things. I was a social media manager at that time, writing social media operating instructions for and overseeing fifteen bases and their social media platforms. As you can imagine, social media was a large part of my life and has always been in a public relations and multimedia field where we were always trying to keep up-to-date with modern communication trends to tell the air force story. I was a social media junkie both on and off duty, as anyone who knows me can attest. And when I returned from the courthouse newly divorced, I did what anyone living in the twenty-first century would do: I posted a brand-new status update about it on my Facebook page.

Once I finished the post, I decided that I would wheel my chair around to my desktop, get on the government secure network, and see what new jobs were available for a single senior master sergeant who wasn't bound by the joint spouse rules anymore. I went to my favorites and clicked on the Assignment Management System link, and the page opened. I did everything I needed to do with the large number of drop-down menus I had to go through to specify my rank, job, and skill level, then clicked submit.

It didn't work at first. Nothing showed up, like what normally happens if you fail to select all the drop-downs properly. At first, I remember thinking that it was just par for the course, that it only made sense the assignment would continue to elude me as it always had. I never fully believed it would be there anyway, but there was a sense of disappointment in that moment, even if only for an instant. I wasn't worried though as I was content with my decision to retire after my deployment anyway. That was my plan.

I was getting ready to close it out, but something told me to try again. We had learned through the years that, when using that system, you had to always try it a few times just to make sure you had done everything right in the drop-downs to confirm there really weren't any jobs out there for you. So I did it again, and a few jobs appeared. Of course, it caught me off guard a little, and I had scrolled down to the bottom of the page somehow before seeing any of the jobs listed. So I scrolled back up to the top and looked at the very first job available.

I'm not sure what happened to me in that moment, but I sure wish I could've been someone else looking at my face at the time. There it was right in front of me—an assignment available to Luke Air Force Base. And for the first time ever, I met *all* the qualifications. It was my dream job in my dream location.

In our career field, we are vectored to certain jobs in certain places based on our career, our education, our performance reports through the years, and the needs of the air force. My career progression was right on track as I had a nearly flawless career and was sitting right where I needed to be. I had been a technician, a supervisor, a section chief, had gone outside the career field to perform a special duty as a first sergeant, and here I was sitting in a headquarters position, just as my career ladder suggested. The only thing left for me on that career ladder was a public affairs superintendent job, and that's exactly what was staring me in the face. My dream job; the top of the ladder in my dream location—a place I had always wanted to go but never thought possible.

Of course, I was in shock. I immediately thought, *Are you kidding me right now?* I didn't think it was real; I didn't think I was looking at what I was looking at. It was supposed to be a joke; it was supposed to be just to see what jobs were out there just for the heck of it.

THE SHELF

This wasn't supposed to happen; this job wasn't supposed to be there. I was ready to retire after my deployment. My kids were here. These are all the things I thought of in what was likely just seconds after realizing it truly was real, and that job truly was sitting right there.

I wheeled my squeaky computer chair around suddenly and yelled to Maja. I said, "Maja, you have to look at this!"

Of course, she was initially sitting there like, *Dude, what?* But as any good friend would do, she wheeled her chair over and looked at the screen. I was locked in on her face, probably because in that moment I just needed someone else to confirm that what I was seeing was there. And sure enough, her eyes got big, and she just said, "Wow."

I had many conversations about faith and God with Maja before that. She wasn't quite the believer that I was, and even I was still new at it. And my faith was still in its infancy, and I was still trying to figure it all out on my own. I wasn't going to church, and I wasn't reading the Bible, but I knew just enough to let God handle things and try not to worry so much about life and all the stumbling blocks that came with it. I had learned enough to speak somewhat smartly about it; and although maybe not interested, Maja would always listen and try to understand how I felt as I walked down this different path of my new journey.

After she said wow, she asked me what I was going to do. My initial instinct was to probably use profanity and be angry that I couldn't go because I already had my mind made up about retiring, but all I could muster in that moment was, "Well, I have to do it, right?" She didn't really know what to say.

I remember sitting there staring at the screen for what seemed like hours, thinking about my retirement plans and thinking about my kids. This move would mess up my plans. I would have to leave my children for two years. I couldn't do it. All these things were racing through my mind, and my brain just wouldn't turn off.

Again, in what seemed like hours, my entire life flashed before my eyes. My kids would be crushed. I was just starting to feel something with Misti, and my relationship with her—or potential for there to be one—would never survive two years apart. My plans—

my plans—would have to change so significantly that it would be more work than it was worth to move and start over and go through all the pain and hurt that would come with it. Why did I even look? Why did it have to be there? Why was I still thinking about actually doing this? I just couldn't close the window. I couldn't stop thinking about it. I just couldn't turn it off.

In all reality, maybe only ten minutes had passed between the time I saw the assignment listed there and having all those thoughts. It was a whirlwind of emotion for sure, with everything I ever knew in my life at that point suddenly getting turned upside down in my mind. I couldn't help it. I knew I had a deployment coming up, and deployments always took priority over permanent assignment changes. But my feeling was strong, and I had to apply for the job. I had to.

So in a moment of clarity and fully trusting in God and what I felt was His will, I clicked submit and applied for the job. Nothing is ever guaranteed at that point, but I applied for it anyway. With how I had started to live my life then as a "baby Christian," I just couldn't deny what I felt God was leading me to do. Some may believe in that, some may not, but I felt that God was pulling the strings, and I had to do my part.

After submitting myself for consideration for the job, I immediately went to my boss and told her what I had done. She was very excited for me and thought I would be a perfect fit for it. Of course, she asked about the deployment and discussed that further with me but said she'd make some calls to see what could be done about it. Deployments always take priority over permanent moves, so the likelihood of their canceling my deployment for me to take this job were slim to none. I knew that going in. I never really thought I'd be the one selected to go.

It wasn't long until my boss called me into her office and told me that the air force assignments people making those decisions would not let me out of my deployment. The deployment was a mission to train African soldiers on how to do our public affairs job. I had performed the same mission for six months in Afghanistan with Afghan soldiers a couple years prior, so they knew I could do the job well because I knew what was expected already. It was only natural that I go. Plus, it was just my turn. There was nothing that could happen to get me out of it, aside from an injury that would prevent me from being able to perform the function, and as a competitive bodybuilder who worked out every day and was in superior shape, the likelihood of that happening was also slim to none. So I was ready to go; it was my turn to deploy.

As nerve-racking as those first couple of days were, I settled down a little and came back to what was my reality prior to looking on the portal for assignments. My boss still wasn't giving up, but she was running into the same roadblocks at every turn about the deployment. It wasn't until the next day that she was told I was the only one who had volunteered for the job. I had no competition; no one else wanted to go. And here I was, so willing to go do a job I'd prepared my whole career for in a place I had always wanted to go. As much as I wanted to get excited about that, I just couldn't. The deployment to Africa was a deal breaker.

My boss told me that she wouldn't give up. They told her that they were going to nonvolunteer someone (or force someone) for the job, and there was nothing they could do. So all hope seemed lost at that point. My boss, of course, was a firecracker and didn't give up on anything that easily. She was a very successful chief master sergeant in one of the highest administrative leadership positions you could be in our career field as a command-level career field manager. She had been around the block or two; and in that position, her job was to take care of people, and that's exactly what she was trying to do for me.

Once she found out about their wanting to non-volunteer someone for the Arizona job, she realized, just as any good leader would, that sending someone to a superintendent position overseeing an entire public affairs office could be a morale killer. The position was a significant one, one that required a person with exemplary leadership and mentoring skills, a person who could lead an entire office filled with people who told the entire air force story of that base to millions of people. Luke Air Force Base was, and still is, the air force's premier combat fighter pilot training base—and was soon to be the home of the United States Armed Forces newest weapon, the F-35 combat fighter jet. There was a significant need here, and my boss knew that sending someone there who didn't want to be there would be a bad idea.

My boss was persistent; she even included our director at the headquarters level and told him she thought it was a bad idea for them to send someone as a nonvolunteer. He agreed and helped with trying to convince the assignments people that they should send me. His involvement and her persistence broke down the barrier a little bit as the Air Force Personnel Center budged and told them that if the Chief of Public Affairs in Arizona would change the dates for when they required the new superintendent to be there, they may consider it.

In the air force, all of what we did when we moved or got deployed was based on the acronym RNLTD, or "report no later than date." The date was significant in that it allowed for transition between the person leaving a position and the new person taking it over. The dates were dictated by those in charge of the gaining unit in need of someone based on their need and the dates the outgoing person would be leaving. And more times than not, leaders making those decisions would never allow someone to come in to take over a position after the predecessor was gone. No turnover generally meant bad news and more time learning the job at first than spent doing it—not something you want to have happen at a superintendent level.

I tell you all that information because I was supposed to leave for my deployment in October for six months, which would have me gone through April. The "report no later than date" for the assignment to Arizona was January 1st—it wasn't even close. And the Chief of Public Affairs at Luke was not going to let the position sit open for four months waiting for me. So my hopes were dashed once again; and as I say that, I don't want you to misunderstand how I was feeling at that time. I never thought it would ever happen to begin with, so I was never disappointed, thinking it wasn't going to happen. But at the same time, it just felt like God had His hands on this somehow; and despite the roadblocks, I felt like He wasn't done working on this just yet. I really can't explain it; it was simply a feeling I had.

THE SHELF

The next day, I came to work with all of this on my mind; but again, there were no real expectations that anything would ever happen or that I would ever go. I walked in that day knowing I had done my part; I applied for the job like I felt God wanted me to. Now, I needed to focus on the fact that I had a deployment to Africa coming up in a couple of months and then retirement to plan after that. I was coming back down to earth and getting back to where I was before I pressed that submit button, and that's when God decided to really show up.

I knew He wasn't done; I knew this wasn't finished. My gut was right as my boss called me into her office and told me my deployment to Africa had just been cancelled. Just as had happened with the same advisory mission I had performed in Afghanistan; the air force was doing away with the advisory mission in Africa. The person that was in place at the time—the same person I had been talking to for a few weeks about what to expect when I got there in October—would be the last person to do the job. There was no longer a need for a replacement. Suddenly, I was no longer being deployed.

Two days later, I had permanent change of station orders for Luke Air Force Base, Arizona. I was friends with the person who matched our public affairs assignments with people, so she told me (on the same day the deployment was cancelled) that I had the job. It just took a couple of days for the permanent change of station orders to flow to make it official and for me to have a hard copy in my hand.

There were so many huge barriers in the way of this change ever happening, yet I watched God work time and time again to enable His will to be done—for His will to be done, not mine; for me to follow His plan, not my own. And suddenly, all I could think about were all those palm trees and all that sunshine! They were the reasons why I had always wanted to get stationed in Arizona in the first place!

But little did I know that God's plan for me had only begun, and my trip to Arizona and Luke Air Force Base was not going to be about palm trees and sunshine. It was going to be something very different—the beginning of an extremely difficult two-year soul-searching journey that would change my life forever. God cleared my path, and I was about to find out why He worked so hard to make sure I was on it.

DAVID K. DEREMER

And Jesus answered them, "Truly, I say to you, if you have faith and do not doubt, you will not only do what has been done to the fig tree, but even if you say to this mountain, 'Be taken up and thrown into the sea,' it will happen."

—Matthew 21:21

CHAPTER 19

Saying Goodbye

The days that followed weren't easy. I told my ex-wife of my upcoming assignment to Arizona, and then, of course, my children. At the time, I didn't think I would ever get anyone to understand my reasons for choosing to leave my children, and some to this day may still not think it was right. But when God speaks and faith kicks in, you don't do anything but follow where you're being led. That's what I did in this case.

Of course, my girls were only told that their daddy had gotten an assignment to Arizona, and that was all they needed to know. It was already hard enough for them without having to hear that I had volunteered for the job. The girls and I did end up talking about it a year later, and they understood, especially after hearing and understanding the rest of the story that you're about to read.

The next step in the process for me was telling Misti that I was going to be leaving. As much as I knew she was in love with me, I knew it would be hard. It was hard on me just thinking about having to tell her, especially since my own feelings for her were growing then too. We weren't really in a relationship then, but things were building up to that. She was my best friend, regardless. Ultimately, I don't remember the conversation being bad or producing tears or anything like that when I finally told her, but I do clearly remember thinking at that time that there was no way we could have a relationship now no matter what I was feeling because it would never work with my being two thousand miles away.

So life went on like it had been because there were still a few months left before I had to leave. We were all just going to enjoy it as best we could while having no idea of what the future was going to hold.

September 2013 and the Kansas City competition came and went. As you read in the previous chapter, I realized I had fallen in love with Misti, so that made leaving even harder as the weeks flew by. She had quickly become the most amazing woman in the world to me, and I was starting to feel an unconditional love like I had never felt before. I was starting to feel as if she truly was my soul mate, the one I had always been looking for, the blessing from God that I had always wanted—or so I thought at the time.

As I said before, my faith was still in its infancy, and I hadn't read the Bible or gone to church much. I just knew to let go, let God lead, and trust in the signs that I was seeing and the good that I felt as a result. At the time, I truly believed she was "the one" and that nothing or no one could ever come between us. And even though I was leaving for Arizona in a couple of months, I tried to remain positive about us. I was still unsure about how it would work; but during those few months I had left, I just stayed positive that it would one way or another. I felt that she was part of God's plan for me; nothing that felt this good could be anything else.

During her time watching me compete, Misti realized that competing was something that she could do too. She was beautiful and driven; there wasn't anything she couldn't do. She had been an athlete her whole life, excelling in basketball, volleyball, and softball in high school. She was small in stature but huge in heart and drive and discipline, with a work ethic unlike anyone I've ever seen—literally like no one I have ever seen. She was fierce, dedicated, disciplined. I never saw her fail at anything. She switched gears from marathons and running to weight lifting and competition preparation and ultimately became the very best at it.

We competed together in a show in St. Louis in October 2013. There had been so much hype in the natural bodybuilding world about my going into that show as I was the up-and-coming newcomer, coming off back-to-back wins and "best poser" awards.

THE SHELF

Coming into the competition in St. Louis, which was practically home turf for us, expectations were high for me in a men's physique class that was still new to bodybuilding. Misti was as prepared as a bikini competitor could be and was a complete natural at it from what I had seen during our posing practice sessions. We had so much fun doing this together. She was ready, and I was so proud.

We took to the stage that day where expectations fell short for me. After back-to-back wins, I placed fourth in the show and was a little disappointed. It was my first taste of real "defeat" despite still being a top five finish.

Misti graced the stage for the first time and just killed it; she was just a true natural. She ended up winning her class and placing second in the overall. But because of the size of the bikini class, they awarded two pro cards that day; she received one of them. So in her first competition, and our first one together, there stood Misti—a brand-new bikini pro.

We went on to compete two more times together before December. Misti always did well, winning just about every show she was in. It had become our thing. I loved being able to be with someone who shared similar interests both in competing itself and the preparation that came along with it. Not everyone can do what it takes to compete, let alone compete, do well, and become pros like we did. So I found myself always being thankful that I had found someone to share it all with. We would just "do what we do," as we'd always say. The memories we created and shared together were so amazing, and they're all things I will remember for the rest of my life.

THE SHELF

The day came for me to leave Illinois for Arizona. I was about to travel two thousand miles across the United States in my car with plenty of time to think about all the things that were about to change. It wasn't easy. I said goodbye to my three girls that morning before they left for school and had plans to meet Misti at the International House of Pancakes (IHOP), which had become our favorite post-competition restaurant to enjoy a cheat meal at after working so hard for so long preparing for stage.

Misti showed up, and we talked for quite a while. I wasn't as invested at the time in our relationship as I would come to be after that, but I knew I loved her, and I knew she loved me too. I didn't want to leave; she didn't want me to leave. I already had regret about the decision I made to volunteer for that job four months prior after seeing the tears in my children's eyes a couple hours before, but I knew I'd be back to see them again. In that moment with Misti though, I wished I had fallen in love with her sooner. There was no way this amazing woman would wait for me, no way I could go that long being alone and lonely without her. Every emotion you can imagine was running through both of us as we sat there that morning, just doing everything we could to delay the inevitable. But the time came: the parking lot goodbye, the flood of tears. All I could do was look back at her in the rearview mirror and just try to convince myself that everything would be okay. Suddenly, in a flash, my best friend was gone.

> For I know the plans I have for you, declares the LORD, plans for welfare and not for evil, to give you a future and a hope.
>
> —Jeremiah 29:11

CHAPTER 20

First Impressions

Traveling to Arizona was so different than anything I had ever experienced before. I actually drove from Illinois to Arizona, so I got to experience many firsts.

I had never seen a cactus before. I had never traveled to a new base alone before. I had never been in the Western United States before. It was the first week of December, and it was eighty degrees with not a single sign of winter in sight. Misti was from California, and I remember wishing that she was there with me as she had told me so much about living out west and the amazing dry heat of the western desert.

My first days in Arizona were like what you would probably expect. Trying to find a place to live, my predecessor giving me the lowdown on the office, getting to know the personnel and my responsibilities in the position, along with figuring out who was who and who did what. I felt I was received well as I have always had that sort of whistle-while-you-work, high-five-you-in-the-hallway type of personality with my subordinates during my career. I've never been one to lead with an iron fist, and my situational style of leading resulted in much success in my career, not only for me but for the offices I led and the many airmen, noncommissioned officers, and senior noncommissioned officers who worked for me.

My first official day in the office was a memorable one; it always will be. I'll never forget the first time I met Tim Boyer. I walked into the office where he ran the base newspaper, and all I heard was rap music. He was seated next to a woman named Deb, a contractor who was responsible for editing the paper and ensuring it was complete for the publisher to print every week for the base and surrounding communities. Tim and Deb would end up being two of the most significant and important people in my life, both having an impact on me that I never knew possible.

Regardless, the rap music got louder as I got closer to Tim's desk. I've always been a Dr. Dre and Snoop Dogg fan over the years, so I didn't have an issue with rap music at all; that wasn't what seemed strange to me. First impressions being what they are, I heard the music, but all noticed that Tim had a degree hanging on the wall behind him—a degree in divinity.

As you can imagine, I was a little confused. Not that I am stereotyping anyone or judging based on their preferred genre of music; but instinctually, it just seemed strange. Not that a Christian man with aspirations of becoming a pastor can't enjoy some good rap music; but again, as an initial instinct, it didn't make sense. (As I'd come to learn later, the rap music playing that day was Lecrae, a Christian rapper, one whom I ended up becoming a huge fan of during my time there with Tim in Arizona.)

My brother Mark joined the air force a couple years after I did; and at the same time I was in Arizona, he was stationed about twelve hours up the coast at Travis Air Force Base and lived in Vacaville, California. This was as close to him as I had been in a few years, even though he and I spent more time being stationed together in the air force than we did growing up (after that day my mother sent me off to be with my father thirty years earlier).

Mark and I were stationed together at Charleston Air Force Base in South Carolina for six years, then again at Kadena Air Base in Japan for three more years. He got to be a part of my kids' lives and help raise them, and I got to be with him and his wife Missy in Japan when they had their first and only daughter, Madison. Looking back now, I realize that God had a plan in place to ensure we'd always keep our bond despite our circumstances. Mark has remained my rock and my best friend for my whole adult life, and I'm so thankful for him and Missy for all they've done for me through the years. It hasn't always been easy, but their unconditional love for me has never once wavered, even during all the times I know I didn't deserve it.

Mark and I were excited about my move to Arizona as it put me within driving distance of Vacaville with Christmas only a few weeks away. Mark and Missy invited me to spend Christmas with them that year since it was my first year really being alone without being able to see my girls. So I took some leave and drove up to Vacaville to spend the holidays with them.

Everything was good. Sun, palm trees, family—it was going to be amazing.

>   For everything there is a season, and a time
>   for every matter under heaven:
>   a time to be born, and a time to die;

THE SHELF

> a time to plant, and a time to pluck up what is planted;
> a time to kill, and a time to heal;
> a time to break down, and a time to build up;
> a time to weep, and a time to laugh;
> a time to mourn, and a time to dance.
>
> —Ecclesiastes 3:1–4

CHAPTER 21

Darkness

The first year in Arizona wasn't an easy one. I dealt with my feelings about Misti and I being apart and with how badly I was missing my kids. I wasn't in a good place. My relationship with Misti was on and off that year too as we both just couldn't seem to find our way in this new situation for many different reasons. And as each day went on that first year, my struggle with it all just seemed to get harder and harder.

It was an exciting time for me at the end of the year, though, as my kids came to Arizona to spend Thanksgiving with me. This was the first time they would come to see me as it was much easier and less expensive for me to fly back to Illinois myself to see them instead. However, this particular year, Misty and I had decided that it would be good for the girls to come to Arizona, and we were all excited about it.

We had an amazing time together while they were there. It was somewhere they had never been, just as it was for me when I first got there, so it made their visit that much more fun for all of us. We didn't travel around much or do anything spectacular, but we played games every night, hung out in the hot tub, and watched movies—all of that in addition to the normal Thanksgiving Day festivities of food and football. Jordan made the most amazing s'mores cupcakes too (didn't want to forget to mention that). That was a process in and of itself, but we had a blast doing it like we did with everything else.

THE SHELF

It's always been the little things that mean the most to me when it comes to them. They never ask for extravagant or expensive things from me, just being together is enough—it's always just been enough. I remember people saying how different I looked in photos I had posted to Facebook while they were there with me and how different I acted when they were around. I never thought too much of it at the time, but it became clear once they left how significant that really was and the impact it would ultimately have on me. My time with them flew by, and the next thing I knew, they were gone.

I walked back into my house after taking them to the airport to fly home, and it was the loneliest I had felt in a long time. It wasn't but a few hours earlier that the house was so full of life with laughs and smiles and hugs and love. And suddenly, just like that, the life was gone; missing—it was dead silent. Glimpses of my girls filled my head, and my eyes filled with tears as I saw signs of them all around. The Phase 10 game box was still on the dining room table, the water bottles were left on the counter, the beds were still unmade in the bedrooms. It was devastating.

The only thing that made it remotely okay was that I had plane tickets and made plans to go back to Illinois a few weeks later to see them before Christmas too, so I knew I'd see them again soon. In the meantime, though, I was miserable. And it was a type of miserable you don't just shake off easily.

My trip back to Illinois around Christmas was not a good one. As I said, Misti and I were on and off a few times during those two years, and we had some issues leading up to my going back there this time as well. So my excitement about the trip back to the Midwest was tempered a little. I didn't feel good about some things as I flew four hours to St. Louis Lambert International Airport. I was uneasy, unsure, and confused. But I got there, got my rental car, and drove to my hotel, just as I had done a few times before when I went back there to visit. I just kept picturing the good things to come with my girls and my getting to play Santa with them for a little while I was there. So I was excited and happy about that and tried to stay as positive as I could about the rest.

Well, "the rest" didn't turn out positive. The issues that Misti and I had leading up to my return to Illinois were too much to overcome at the time. We met to talk about things and decided that it was best for us both to call it quits. It wasn't easy; it was one of the most difficult moments in my life as she was still my soul mate in my mind. There were many things we didn't see eye to eye on and many other details that really don't need to be shared here. At the time, we just did what we thought was best for us no matter how hard it was. That was that.

My time with the girls was amazing, though, and I was able to take each of them shopping and spoil them for Christmas since I wouldn't be there on the actual day. We had fun; we always did.

The plane ride home after that was long. Because it hadn't been long since the girls were there for Thanksgiving, my thoughts of their being there were still alive and well in my mind and in my heart. I didn't really understand the magnitude of what was going on inside of me until I walked in the door of my house—this time without my kids and without Misti. It hit me quick, and it hit me hard. I fell to my knees in tears with a broken heart and a complete and total misery that I had never felt before. I hurt everywhere, and the entire world as I knew it was crashing in on me. I was completely broken.

Of course, Tim knew about my situation with Misti; and as an aspiring pastor and devout Christian, he had always kept it real with me about how wrong our relationship was while she was still in a marriage, even if she knew it was over and her divorce was imminent. Tim's reasons for saying the things he would always say were justified by God and the Bible, of course, but my free will and my love for her controlled my decision-making for a long time, no matter what some would consider to be wrong.

Initially, my plan was to try and sleep Christmas day away since I had no family there. I had already spent the year prior with my brother, and I thought he needed to just have Christmas with his own family without big brother hanging around again. Of course, Tim wasn't having any of that as he and his wife, Jaycee, treated me like family and were always there when I needed them. They invited me into their home for Christmas, and I hesitantly accepted because I felt it was a day for people to spend with their own families, and I didn't want to feel like I was intruding. However, after much discussion, I decided it just would give me an opportunity to play Santa again, so I took advantage of the opportunity to have fun with it while loading up a large bag full of presents for Tim's kids and taking it with me when I went over there.

Christmas was great. I enjoyed my time with Tim and his family, but things inside me still weren't right or good. I was nearing a rock bottom I had never experienced before; and the closer the New Year came, the more it reminded me of the previous New Year I spent with Misti. I missed her; every day, my heart ached more and more, and I began to sink lower and lower. I could feel myself completely falling apart. I had little interest in work or people or anything. I felt trapped; I felt alone; I felt like someone I had never been before.

I ended up going to sleep at around nine o'clock on New Year's Eve just because I wanted it all to go away: the holidays, the New Year's Eve hype—everything. I just kept telling myself that everything was going to be better in 2015. It was an opportunity for me to have that new start everyone seems to feel can happen—just like that—once midnight hits. Of course, it's never that easy.

My emotions had started to truly get the best of me at this point, and I was starting to think about things I had never thought about before. I missed my kids terribly; I missed Misti and my morning "good morning, handsome" texts. I had already been to the emergency room for severe chest pains where there was initial fear of a possible heart attack; but ultimately, there was nothing concrete to support that diagnosis. I was in the hospital for three days with doctors scratching their heads. There was something abnormal in one of the EKGs that had been done the first day, which prompted them to admit me; but ultimately, I was released with a clean bill of health, and that was that. The fact that I was in such good shape likely prevented things from being worse. Stress is a dangerous thing.

A week after I got out of the hospital for that, I was back in for an extensive sinus surgery that had been planned prior to my earlier trip to the emergency room for the chest pains. I was so anxious to get this surgery done as I was beginning to have so many issues with breathing and sinus infections. It was a hereditary thing as my father, mother, and brother all had multiple sinus surgeries each to fix their own various sinus issues; it was only a matter of time until it was my turn. In addition, they discovered in my allergy tests that I was severely allergic to dust and also allergic to practically the entire state of Arizona, so my issues would only get worse if I didn't have the surgery done right then.

The surgery went well. Tim was right there for me—literally, this time—and I was able to stay at his house that night since I was unable to drive. My nostrils had stents in them and were also packed full of stuffing and gauze. In addition to that, the entire outside of my nose was covered to stop me from bleeding all over. It didn't bother me really. I was loaded with narcotics, with friends who always made me feel comfortable, and feeling good. No big deal.

I went home the next day, and that's when life came crashing down on me again. This time, it was a rock bottom depth like you can't imagine. I ended up being home for almost six weeks after my surgery when two weeks was the normal recovery time. An infection had spread throughout my body, causing me to feel severe flu-like symptoms nonstop for more than a month. The doctors changed medications three times, and nothing seemed to work. It was clear to me that my body was just going to have to push it out over time, and I'd have to suffer—and suffer is exactly what I did.

THE SHELF

What made things worse for me was that life just didn't turn off while I was recovering from surgery. I still missed my kids; I still missed Misti too, and our now being broken up was really triggering my insecurities, and thoughts of her potentially being with other people was tearing me apart. I was alone and miserable—physically, mentally, emotionally, and spiritually miserable. I was headed to a very dark place, and there was nothing anyone could do about it.

I'll never forget the night it happened. As I said before, my nose was packed full. It didn't bother me at Tim's house that first night, but it had started to bother me after that as the infection was making me feel so horrible. I started having panic attacks. I would jump out of bed in the middle of the night and feel like I was suffocating. I ripped every bit of stuffing out of my nose that I could. I was miserable, I was suffering, and I experiences all that while, in that moment, I felt as if I had lost everything: my kids, my soul mate, my purpose—everything.

I reached for my bottle of narcotics and then remember seeing myself in the mirror. My initial intent when grabbing the bottle was to just take the one for the pain in my nose. But as I stood there looking at myself with a full bottle in my hand, all I saw was someone completely battered and broken. Every part of me felt destroyed; every piece of me was shattered; every memory I had in that moment produced more and more tears. Finally, as the world seemed to be crashing down all around me, seven words I never thought I'd ever consider saying came to me: *I don't want to do this anymore.*

DAVID K. DEREMER

Suicide isn't just something fake you see on television or in the movies—it's real. I never thought I'd ever be in a situation in my life where I'd think, even for a second, about wanting to die. But there I was, staring at myself in the mirror, ready to end it all. It wasn't a good feeling; it was dark and cold and lonely. I knew that doing this could make all the pain go away.

Thankfully, there were three things that stood in my way that day, three things between me and a stomach full of narcotics that likely would have ended my life. Those three things were Logan, Jordan, and Allison. I was one of the lucky ones. Even as I stood there broken and battered on every level imaginable, I was able to recognize that the pain I was going through as I stood there that night was nothing compared to the lifetime of pain I would put my children through if I had swallowed all those pills and died. I was able to recognize that my thoughts were selfish, and I was able to recognize that I really needed help.

> Fear not, for I am with you;
> be not dismayed, for I am your God;
> I will strengthen you, I will help you,
> I will uphold you with my righteous right hand.
>
> —Isaiah 41:10

CHAPTER 22

Getting Help

The lobby was full of people, everyone with their heads down, buried in papers on clipboards to fill out. As I walked in the doors, I noticed two women behind desks and two counter-to-ceiling-length walls of glass. There was just enough space between us and them to pass papers through. I remember thinking about the reasons why the window was built that way. Those reasons weren't good ones, especially in this place. I just stood there thinking, *How did I end up here?*

In the air force, the section of the hospital where people go for these types of problems—drug abuse, alcohol treatment, depression, anxiety, PTSD—was commonly referred to as the "mental health" clinic. Over the years, it was generally regarded as a place you didn't want to go because then the air force would have documentation of whatever issues you had. The common misconception was that any visit there would impact your career. While I never had any reason to go there in my previous twenty-one years in the air force, I do remember hearing all the stories. Of course, most of the misconceptions weren't true, and resources such as these were in place to truly help people.

As I sat there in the lobby filling out paperwork, I did end up feeling a little uncomfortable. The stigma of being in that place was fresh in my mind; and suddenly, I felt like I had a huge label on me as being one of "those guys." Especially as a senior master sergeant—a senior leader in charge of an office of twenty-five people.

Despite what I knew, despite how much I knew this place could help, I couldn't help feeling the way I did about it in that moment.

But as quickly as I thought that, I also thought about my kids. They were why I was there; and at the end of the day, I didn't care what anyone thought about seeing me there. I was there to fix me, so I would be around for them—and "them" has always been more important to me than anything else in the world.

A short older woman came to the door and called out my name that first day and took me back to her office, closed the door, and told me I could sit down. It was everything you would generally imagine a psychologist's office would be, even equipped with the couch you'd commonly see people on TV lying on when they made visits to their "shrink." Of course, I didn't lie down or anything, but I did sit on the couch every time as the doctor sat beside the couch on her chair with her doctorate degree perched just above her head on the wall. I'm big on credibility when it comes to trusting people and sources, so I immediately noticed that and felt comfortable. As apprehensive as I was to be diving into this and doing something new that would make me so completely vulnerable, I felt okay. I needed help, I reached out, I was there—it would be okay.

The first session was hard. I cried profusely as I talked about missing my children and Misti. I explained everything to her in general that day, from the kids leaving, to the surgery, to the issues in

THE SHELF

my relationship, and everything in between. It was a start, but we hadn't even scratched the surface, I'd come to find out later. There was so much more going on with me than I ever knew; and over the next year, we would break down all the barriers to discovering exactly what they were.

Casting all your anxieties on him because he cares for you.

—1 Peter 5:7

CHAPTER 23

Baptism

As luck would have it, having an aspiring pastor as a subordinate would end up being a great thing for me. Not only would Tim become an amazing friend to me, but he became a spiritual mentor and my guide on this new journey I decided to embark on. He had an influence on my life in a different way than anyone had ever had before. God used Tim as the vessel to help me, to educate me, to sometimes beat me down and break me to build me up again. Despite my being his boss, Tim didn't pull punches with me when it came to the Scriptures, what I was doing, and how he felt about it. It was this truth, honesty, credibility, and a genuine concern for my future that drew me to him in the first place.

Tim and his family went to a church called Christ's Church of the Valley and got me to start going with them. It had been a very long time since I'd been in the church on a regular basis, so being there in a new, modern environment was amazing. I loved everything about it, and it felt like home. I was learning a lot there; but it was Tim who was the captain of the ship I was on, chartering my course to different places in a slow, meaningful manner so I could be in the best possible place when it came to faith and understanding it all the right way.

I had been a hypocrite for a very long time. I was the guy who would think I could sin, and it would be okay because God would forgive me, then just continue to do the same things wrong and sin over again the next day. It wasn't true faith, nor did I really have a good grasp on what being a true Christian was like. At this point

THE SHELF

though, I had started to make a very significant change and wasn't quite a hypocrite anymore. However, I still had much to learn.

I remember the biggest turning point for me during that journey. It's almost embarrassing to talk about now, but since I'm totally raw and exposed here anyway, a little humor for you at my expense will probably just add to the entertainment value. Tim would tell me all the time that I needed to get in my Bible. He'd tell me every day all the answers were there, and I needed to get inside of it and read it and understand it. He was right, but I had a problem.

I was standing in his office talking about the Bible and faith and having one of our normal conversations. Here I am, a forty-year-old man with a pretty good education and enough life experience for probably ten people. I remember Tim asking me again if I had been in my Bible. I talked my way around it a little; but that day, he was seeing right through me. He just kept on me over and over about needing to get in my Bible, until I finally told him, *"I would love to read it. But when I do, I can't understand what any of it means!"*

You see, I had an old Bible that was handed down to me when my grandmother died. It was an old King James Version, likely printed long before study Bibles and new translation Bibles were available. My problem was, I was aware of these other translations and didn't know you could get a Bible written differently so the message was more clear and easier to understand. Once Tim told me about them, I felt so dumb. He kind of laughed at me, we got online, and he told me which one to get. Of course, then I became excited. I could finally read this thing, understand it, and finally start to make some sense of all the Bible wisdom he would speak of all the time.

That Bible changed everything: my view on faith, my understanding—everything. It tied together all the bits and pieces I had heard over the years and everything Tim had told me up to that point. Suddenly, things were starting to make sense, from the beginning when Jesus walked on the earth as a man turning water into wine to the empty tomb and His rising from the dead. Suddenly, things were starting to make sense. I craved knowledge; I started to feel different. It got to the point where I couldn't wait to get home, dive in that Bible, and read more to see what was going to happen next. *This is what I've been missing all this time,* I often thought to myself each night as I sat in my hot tub so fully engrained in the Word and this new life I was so anxiously wanting to live.

It wasn't long after that when Tim finally talked to be about baptism; he had a plan, I think. Tim wanted me to fully understand things so when the time came for me to be baptized, I'd know exactly what I was doing. He did what any Christian should do when trying to bring a new soul to Christ. His plan worked to perfection because when that day came to talk about it all, I didn't hesitate. I was ready for this life change. I was ready to give myself to the Lord and become a better man and have all my problems go away. But that was my first mistake—thinking that baptism would make all the bad stuff go away, or that it would make life easier.

I was baptized by Tim on a sunny Arizona day in June at our church. Friends were there to watch as Tim dunked me in the water and pulled me back out as someone who had just given his life to the Lord. In that instant, I felt different, changed, optimistic. It was an amazing day, and I was thankful for it; I still am. I remember thinking about how much my life was going to change, and I was finally going to become the man that I knew in my heart I always wanted to be. I was happy with that; I was ready for it. I couldn't wait to see what the world had to offer me now.

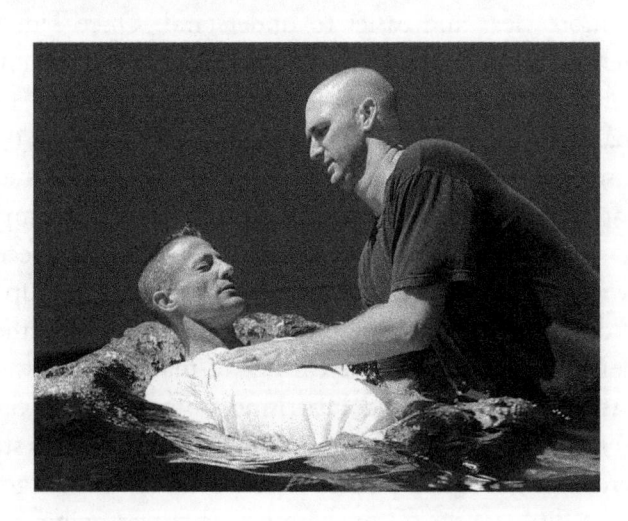

THE SHELF

As it turned out, all the magic didn't happen like I thought it would. The days that came after that were long; the days that came after that were hard. While I never lost faith in God or abandoned Him, I struggled. I had made a huge mistake thinking that everything would just be amazing without much effort after that.

As time went on and I stayed in the Bible and learned more, I came to understand the reasons for my struggle. I was now being held to a higher standard in God's eyes. Sin was viewed differently. Whenever I did anything wrong or even thought anything wrong, I felt like I was disappointing Him. The feelings I had were intensified so much after being baptized. It was hard at first; but the more I learned, the easier it got. I am not a saint and will never proclaim to be, but I am a Christian, and I'm one because I know I sin and need Jesus in my life more than anyone. That was what I had to learn. He knows we sin, and He's there to forgive you and help you on the path to be better and do better. And that's what I always tried to do. I had so much going on inside of me, both good and bad, but God always kept my head above water and kept me hanging on. In my world, where some days it just felt like the pain was never going to end, God at least made it okay to get out of bed in the morning and keep trying.

God gave me hope; God provided for me even in the darkest of times. I found peace in that, and it was then that I finally realized why God created a path for me that led to Arizona. He knew my heart, He knew who I wanted to be, and He knew the next step on my journey was there in Arizona: to meet Tim and Deb, to learn, and to find the God that I so desperately wanted to find—to find Him, have a relationship with Him, and allow Him to break me down and build me up again the right way—to be surrounded by amazing people who could support me along the way.

This was my defining moment. God made this all possible that day when He put that job on the assignment board to Arizona and cancelled my deployment to Africa. My move to Arizona was never about sun and palm trees; it was about starting on a real journey with God and doing it with the right people around me.

DAVID K. DEREMER

And you will know the truth, and the truth will set you free.

—John 8:32

CHAPTER 24

PTSD, Abandoholism, and Me

I discovered so much about myself during counseling. I was initially diagnosed with major depressive disorder and severe anxiety as those symptoms were glaring right from the start for my doctor and my counselor. After the first visit, my primary care doctor started me on antidepressants—another thing I never thought I'd have to do; but because my depression and anxiety were so severe, I had to.

The descriptions for each illness described my daily life right down to the letter, from the loss of pleasure in doing things, to the feeling of just wanting to be alone and my strong desire to isolate myself from the world. It was an eye-opening experience to understand that I was now a man with significant issues to deal with, yet I still had no real idea why I had them or how to overcome them.

As it turned out, there was way more to it than just depression and anxiety; and as time went on, we were finally able to get to the root cause of my issues. I was diagnosed with PTSD a little while after counseling had started; and at that point, we really began to dive in to the root causes of it. My type of PTSD was considered lesser known—an abandonment form of PTSD that I will explain in further detail later in this chapter.

We discovered that suppressing early childhood trauma for almost forty years resulted in an emotional imprint on my psychobiological functioning. And it wasn't until the separation from my own children for the first time and my breakup with Misti that the severity of it broke me down completely, triggered those suicidal thoughts, and ultimately led me to seek counseling. I thank God every day for having those thoughts, as odd as that may sound, because I know that without them, I may have never realized or ever discovered the severity of what was really happening. The abandonment crisis going on inside me had negatively impacted so many of the decisions and choices I had made for my entire adult life, and I never even knew it.

For you to have a better understanding of how this all ties together with me, it's important for you to know that PTSD of abandonment is a psychobiological condition in which earlier separation traumas end up interfering with your current life. The most glaring sign of this significant interference in one's life is extremely intrusive anxiety, which often manifests itself into feelings of insecurity, promoting self-sabotage in the primary relationships in our life. In addition, it interferes with our sometimes being able to achieve long-range goals. Fortunately for me, I never had many issues reaching long-range professional goals I had set for myself; it was always the personal side that seemed to have suffered.

Another glaring sign of PTSD of abandonment is the tendency to compulsively reenact our abandonment scenarios through repetitive patterns, also known as "abandoholism" or being attracted to the unavailable.

Abandoholism is like other "holisms," but instead of being addicted to substance, you're addicted to the emotional drama of having your heart broken. You seek hard-to-get lovers to keep the romantic intensity going and to keep your body's love chemicals and stress hormones flowing. To sum it up, with what we face every day, abandoholism sets in when you've been hurt so many times that you've come to equate insecurity with love. So unless you're interested or seeking someone that you're insecure about, you often don't feel in love.

Conversely, when that special person comes along who wants to be with you, that person's availability often fails to arouse the required level of insecurity you need. And if you can't feel those yearning, lovesick feelings, then you don't always feel the attraction and continue to pursue different, unavailable partners. You become psychobiologically addicted to the high-stakes drama of an emotional challenge and the love-chemicals that go with it.

Abandoholism is driven by fear of abandonment. When you're significantly attracted to someone, it almost immediately arouses fear of losing that person; this fear sometimes causes you to become insecure. You try to hide your insecurity, but your desperation often shows through, causing your partners to lose an interest in you or causing them to just become so exhausted with trying to pick you up, make you comfortable or reassure you that they can't do it anymore. That was what happened with Misti and me at many points in our relationship. Abandoholics tend to swing back and forth between fear of abandonment and fear of engulfment. You're either pursuing hard-to-get-lovers or you're feeling turned off my someone who actually is interested in you.

Conversely, abandophobics are so afraid of being rejected that they avoid being in relationships altogether. Abandophobics act out their fear of abandonment by remaining socially isolated or by appearing to search for someone when in fact they are pursuing people who are unattainable or not pursuing anyone at all. They do this simply to avoid the risk of getting attached to a real prospect, someone who they feel might abandon them sooner or later.

There is a little abandophobism in every abandoholic. It's true as there's a small amount of abandophobia in me too. But the overarching takeaway here is that, for both abandoholics and abandophobics, a negative attraction is often more compelling than a positive one.

These patterns of attraction and abandonment may have been cast in childhood; and if you've read all my story up to this point, you can already see that this all applies to me. You struggled to get more attention from your parents or significant adult figures in your young life and were left feeling unfulfilled; this caused you to doubt your self-worth. Over time, your craving for approval is internalized, and you learn to idealize others at your own expense, and this becomes a pattern in your love-relationships. Now as an adult, you recreate this scenario by giving your love partners all the power, elevating them above yourself. This recreates the old familiar yearnings you grew accustomed to as a child. Feeling emotionally deprived and "less than" is what you've come to expect.

But why does insecurity linger? Recent scientific research shows that rather than dissipate, fear tends to incubate, gaining intensity over time. That's what happened to me with Misti while I was in Arizona. Insecurity increases with each romantic rejection, causing you to look to others for something you've become too powerless to give yourself: esteem. When you seek acceptance from a withholding partner, you place yourself in a one-down position, recreating the unequal dynamics you have with your parents or peers; you choreograph this scenario over and over. Conversely, you are unable to feel anything when someone freely admires or appreciates you.

This abandonment compulsion is insidious. You didn't know it was developing; until now, you didn't have a name for it. Abandoholism is a new concept. Welcome to my world!

Another example of abandonment trauma is suffering from a diminished self-esteem and an increased fear of vulnerability in social situations, including the workplace. This vulnerability immediately intensifies our need to put our walls up, or strengthen our already-existing walls, with the intent to protect ourselves from further rejection, criticism, or abandonment. Of course, for me, those defenses became a habit and ended up doing more harm than good for me because they created emotional tension and often ruined connections I had with Misti and many others.

My counselor told me that my feelings and ways of adjusting were due to the abandonment I had experienced as a child but never confronted. It was a significant part of why my first engagement would never become more than what it was and helped contribute to the ultimate demise of my marriage. Of course, I made many poor choices and won't blame everything bad that's happened in my life on PTSD; but if I had known then what I know now, it may have changed some things. But who am I to question any of it or the reasons why it all happened? God had a plan for me, and this was all a part of it.

> Not only that, but we rejoice in our sufferings, knowing
> that suffering produces endurance, and endurance
> produces character, and character produces hope.
>
> —Romans 5:3–4 (ESV)

CHAPTER 25

Military Muscle

My time spent in the natural bodybuilding world competing created many opportunities for me. I had sponsors and received so many e-mails and requests to represent different brands of supplements, pills, and apparel. I had been on the cover of a magazine, people talked about me on radio shows, and my stage photos were all over the place after winning back-to-back shows and "Best Poser" awards early in my bodybuilding career. As the popularity of the men's physique class of bodybuilding grew, so did my own.

Military Muscle was an online fitness community that had followers all over the world. Not only was Military Muscle a social media platform for military fitness enthusiasts to follow, the company also sold limited fitness apparel and gear on its website. Most of the people I knew, who knew about Military Muscle, knew them as the company who did "shout-outs" on their Instagram and Facebook pages for random military service members. People would submit their fitness-related photos to the e-mail provided; and each day (sometimes more than once per day), the Military Muscle people would post a submission to their page. It was something that people just fell in love with and, as time went by, something I had grown to follow on a consistent basis before finally deciding to submit a photo myself.

As luck would have it, Robert, the co-owner of Military Muscle, had just retired from the air force out of Luke Air Force Base, where I was, and was still living in the local area. I happened to know a girl who did photo shoots for Military Muscle to advertise their apparel; and a few months before the New Year, she said something to Robert about my being stationed there, and that I was a men's physique pro. She also told him that I may be a good person to consider bringing in as a sponsored athlete for Military Muscle.

Robert reached out once to discuss the possibility, but it was more of a conversation about when to sit down and talk about it more than it was doing so. Then, later in the year, he contacted me to tell me they wanted to bring me in as a sponsored athlete for sure. He said we'd get together sometime to talk about specifics after I asked him for some time to sit down and discuss my role and what they'd expect from me. That's just how I've always been as a subordinate and as a leader. Things always run more efficiently and effectively when everyone knows exactly what it is they're supposed to be doing and know what's expected of them.

THE SHELF

The holidays came and went, and I didn't hear any more about it from Robert. I had started promoting myself on my own social media platforms for the company, and Robert had invited me to go with him to a TheFitExpo in Los Angeles where Military Muscle would have a booth for the very first time as a company. I wasn't sure about going at the time as I was dealing with my depression and anxiety and still struggling to fight off the infection that was running rampant through my body following my surgery. I could barely get off the couch to go to the bathroom without pain and exhaustion most days during that time. In the meantime, as I lay there bored, watching television, I would mess around with photos and graphics on my phone and computer to create posts promoting Military Muscle as one of their sponsored athletes.

Once I started doing that and posting to my Facebook and Instagram pages, my following blew up. For me, multimedia, graphics, photography, social media, and everything associated with multimedia had been my life for more than twenty years. Public affairs, marketing, and social media was what I did every day in the air force. I'm passionate about it; I love it; I'm great at it. And Robert noticed—that's when he called me.

During the telephone conversation, I told Robert that I just had surgery and was home and off work for a few weeks. I didn't get into details of how horrible I was feeling or all the other things I was dealing with in my life at the time, but Robert seemed genuinely interested in talking to me right away. Because he only lived a short distance away and would be in my area that day, he told me that if it was okay and easier for me, he would just stop by my house, and we could sit and discuss things.

Now, with my truly isolating myself from people while dealing with everything that had happened in the previous year, I was hesitant but remember feeling comfortable with Robert, his sincerity as a person, and who he appeared to be. Plus, I thought that maybe being at home in my comfort zone would help with any anxiety I might have. So I agreed to meet him at home, gave him my address, and he showed up at my front door about an hour later.

We talked for two hours about everything, from my life as a competitive professional natural bodybuilder to everything I had done to promote myself for Military Muscle on my social media pages. Prior to this conversation, Robert had no idea what I had done in the air force for more than twenty years, nor did he know that in my job before coming to Arizona, I provided social media training and operating instructions for hundreds of people in the public affairs career field on fifteen different bases in our command. Social media was my wheelhouse, and I knew all the ins and outs, peak times, how to post and when, and every other possible way to use the power of social media to promote anything—people, business, or otherwise.

As Robert would tell the story to me later, he walked out of my house, walked down the sidewalk to his truck while calling the other co-owner Elijah, and the first thing Robert told him was, "You know that marketing person I told you we needed and have been missing? I think I just found him." And that conversation between those two would soon be the beginning of an amazing journey for me, one that I so desperately needed at a time in my life when I felt I had nothing else.

We did end up going to TheFitExpo, Los Angeles; and later, we would find that it was the launching point to a brand-new start for Military Muscle. I rode with Robert from Arizona to Los Angeles, and we talked at length about different things that had to do with Military Muscle, from apparel to marketing. He threw out the term "chief marketing officer" and discussed how they really needed a professional to do their marketing to propel the company forward. I was intrigued but wasn't going with him to the expo to be their professional marketer; I was going as one of their sponsored athletes.

The weekend was an amazing success; we couldn't have asked for more. Inside, I was still dying mentally and emotionally and physically. I felt awful the whole weekend (imagine being on your feet for three days straight with the worst possible flu you've ever had), but there was something in Robert and Elijah that weekend that really pulled me out of my funk a little. It felt good, and I hadn't felt good in a very long time.

On the drive back from the expo, Rob asked me if I wanted to take on the new chief marketing officer role, and I gladly accepted. The months that followed were amazing. Suddenly, I had a goal, I had a purpose, and I had something to do to keep my mind occupied and off missing my kids and off my breakup with Misti. Every day, I started to feel better and better, and it seemed like there was a light—albeit a very faint one—at the end of the tunnel for me.

As we grew as a company, my own social media following grew. People were inspired by me; people were inspired by us; people were motivated by us. The Military Muscle mission and vision I would end up writing and posting on the website took on a life of its own. Suddenly, we were more than just an apparel company and an online fitness community of "meatheads" and bikini girls; we were a company known for supporting people, mentoring people, and motivating and inspiring people. It was amazing the number of lives we were helping, changing, and in some cases saving.

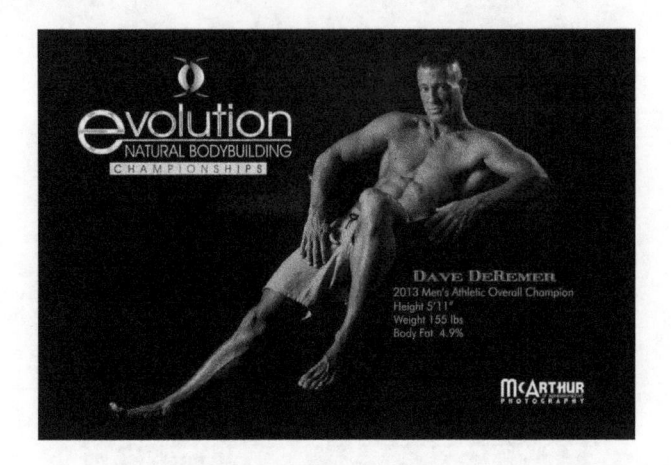

At the end of January, Misti reached out to me. Apparently, some of my posts about having surgery and being in the hospital had made their way to her, and she was concerned, so she called me. She was upset that I hadn't contacted her to talk about it all, which was surprising to me because I thought we were over, and that she wouldn't care or want to know. I really didn't want sympathy, especially from her, so maybe I just didn't think she needed to know. Regardless, she reached out.

We talked a little bit, and that was that. There was no reconciliation at all, but it was obvious that there were still real feelings there; and what I didn't realize at the time was that those feelings, our relationship, and my internal struggles with PTSD would ultimately end up impacting my relationships with everyone at Military Muscle.

There were so many good times about Military Muscle that I could go into detail about and probably write a book about itself. But in keeping with the theme of the book, I'll fast-forward to the late summer and early fall when I was preparing for retirement in mid-October. Robert and I started to have many serious conversations about what I was going to do. At the time, Military Muscle was going to be my life and my future. I had found my place, and this was what I wanted to do with the rest of my life. Of course, we were a small company that was really starting to take off and find its way; but in terms of company sales, we had essentially started over and become a brand-new start-up company with a new vision, one that wasn't prepared to start paying out five- or six-figure salaries to the people working in it. That included people about to retire from the military who needed one of those types of salaries to pay the bills—people like me.

You see, for the time that I worked with Military Muscle, I never got paid. Sure, I got free T-shirts, and Robert always felt like that was enough for the extensive amount of work I was doing and the responsibilities I had, but there was no regular income for me. I was only a "chief marketing officer" in name; I wasn't making an income like a company executive would make in the "real world" with the same title. I knew that was the case going in though; and when it all started, I didn't care about that. I was getting way more out of being a part of the company than money at that time. Of course, I had no idea that we would do the things we did in the six months that followed, but Military Muscle was pulling me out of a funk most didn't know I was in, and I was good with how things were in the beginning; I now had a purpose. I didn't have a need at the time for them to pay me for what I was doing.

But as the days got closer to retirement, and I had to start making some serious decisions, I started hinting to Robert that I needed to know what we were going to do. I kept hinting that I couldn't spend the time doing that job for free after retirement and still be able to pay my bills—that was just real life. It was never about the money for me, but Robert and others always took it that way. They never seemed to understand that I just couldn't survive spending fifty to sixty hours per week doing a job for nothing when I had bills to pay. It was okay when I was in the air force but wouldn't be when I retired. Retirement pay is not *that* much.

So as time went by, retirement got closer, and I really had to start dropping more hints—the animosity and resentment started. I was told I'd be taken care when retirement time came, and it just wasn't happening. Nor do I think they ever really had a plan to make it happen.

Once I realized that, things got rough for Robert and me; Elijah and I already didn't get along. Every company has drama, and no one was really to blame for most of ours, but with there being some already-existing issues, it didn't help things with Robert and me in the end when it came to Military Muscle, the future, and where my place was moving forward. I was still a part of it when I retired and left Arizona, but the relationships were strained, and there was never a resolution to the money situation. At the end of the day, Robert wanted me to continue to do the same things I was doing before, and I wasn't going to do so without some sort of pay commensurate with responsibility. I wasn't greedy at all, but I had done so much to positively impact the monthly sales and revenue of the company that it felt like all my work and efforts were starting to be taken advantage of.

After I retired and moved home, Robert and I talked a few times at first, and I was still a part of the company as I had been. However, I was starting to look for jobs and rethinking my role in the company. I told Robert that I just couldn't continue to do what he expected of me. Of course, he didn't like it, and I assume he was anticipating my saying so as some of my administrative rights on the company Facebook page had already been removed. So I knew they were preparing for it. Our conversation ended well, and he said he still wanted me to be a part of the team even if my title and role changed. Robert left things okay; Robert left things friendly. The relationship was still intact, and I was still a part of the company that pulled me out of my funk nine months prior.

I'm not sure what was going on with me after that. I talked bad about the situation with one of our Military Muscle representatives—someone I thought I could vent to and trust—and talked about company income and other things I never should have shared. Here I was, after just having a good conversation with Robert, bashing the company, how I felt about them not valuing my worth, and divulging information that one of our company representatives didn't have any business knowing. Looking back now, I wish I could take it all back; but of course, I can't. I often wonder if I was sabotaging that relationship before they could let me go, but there's no way to tell if it was that or if I was just frustrated and venting about things I shouldn't have been. In the end, I just own it. I was in the wrong.

That was the end of my time with Military Muscle. While things didn't end all that well, I'll always be grateful for that time and for my friends being available when I needed them. I wasn't in the greatest of places when it all started, but we did so much good during that time. Being a part of Military Muscle gave me a purpose, a reason to get up in the morning, a reason to smile. I'll never forget the good times I had as a part of it or the fact that Robert, Elijah, and Military Muscle may have been the very things that saved my life.

> Do not neglect to do good and to share what you have, for such sacrifices are pleasing to God.
>
> —Hebrews 13:16

CHAPTER 26

The Calling

I retired in mid-October 2015. My girls were there for the ceremony, along with my brother Mark. We all had such a blast for those couple of days, and I was on cloud nine about finally being able to hang up my boots and uniform for good. Mark had retired a year prior and had always talked to me about how amazing it was. I couldn't wait for it to finally happen to me; and when it did, it was a freedom like I could have never imagined. After all, my entire adult life had been spent in the military, and I knew nothing else; I knew no other way to live. I was excited about the future and what life would be like outside of the air force.

THE SHELF

Mark and the girls left after the ceremony, and I left Arizona for good a few days later once all my retirement out-processing was completed. I was excited to finally be going home to my three beautiful baby girls. I had pictured what it was going to be like for so long. The girls were older, and one of them was already off to college. I knew they'd have crazy schedules with school and sports and boys, and my time with them would be limited, but I was still excited to be going home to them anyway.

As the months went by leading up to my retirement, Misti and I talked more and more, and things slowly started moving back in the right direction. She told me she wanted me to come home to her, and I just remember being optimistic about my life once and for all.

I got back to Illinois and found a beautiful home for rent that was more than four thousand square feet, had four bedrooms, five bathrooms, a huge kitchen, two living rooms, three dining rooms, and a sunroom overlooking a large lake in the backyard. My decision to rent this home was always with the thought that there may end up being more people eventually living with me when I got home; that never ended up being the case. But it did have a lake full of fish, and I had a paddleboat to use to go out and catch them. I spent so much time on that lake thinking about my life, my kids, my relationship, my future, and writing a book.

While in that house, I felt a strong calling from God to share my story. I was watching one of the live television shows about the life of Christ one night and started getting strong feelings about all the things I had been through in my life. It was one of those strange, different feelings that you can't deny. And after all the things that had happened in my life those couple of years prior, I knew who was causing them and what that person was trying to tell me. In that moment, I had visions of all the amazing things God had done for me, despite all the bad things I had gone through in my life from childhood until then. It was clear to me in that moment that I had a story to tell, and God wanted me to share it with the world, so I just started writing.

I wrote for hours and hours every single day. It was an emotional roller coaster to have to relive so many memories of my life, both good and bad. Some days were harder than others. Some days, I questioned whether it was truly God's will for me to write at all or if it was just something I was doing on my own. Some days, it was therapeutic. Some days, it was absolutely amazing. And some days, I was just lost.

As I was about four chapters short of finishing the first draft manuscript, so many thoughts of the past were flooding my brain and heart. After days of writing, I was exhausted both physically and mentally. It got so emotional at times, and I often found myself questioning all the things that had happened over the years, my PTSD, and all my relationships. In addition to all that, I started to question whether I was really supposed to write it all, as I said. Initially, I started writing this because I felt called by God to do it so my story could help others. So when I had doubts about it and struggled with wondering if it was really meant for me to do, it bothered me. I didn't want to go against what God wanted of me. I didn't want my free will and worry to overshadow His will and what was meant to be. But I questioned it; it bothered me. And because of those things, I struggled to continue writing anymore.

After the relationship with Misti ended, I found myself questioning the book and its true purpose even more. I went back and forth every single day. I suddenly got writer's block. I sat down to write but couldn't find any words—none, and that was rare for me. I felt helpless. I wasn't sure what to do. I had already poured my heart out for fifteen chapters or so and had more than one hundred pages in my manuscript, and now I was questioning it? Now I was wondering if there would ever be an end to the story.

So I did what I always do—I prayed. I prayed for clarity and guidance and wisdom and strength. I woke up the next morning, and like I always do, I praised the Lord for giving me another day and asked Him to guide me through my day. In addition to that, I prayed about the book and just asked for a sign that it was truly His will for me to be writing it. I didn't want to do it for my own selfish desires or for recognition; I wanted to do it because I knew there was a purpose that was far bigger than me—a purpose that may help others by promoting awareness for a lesser-known form of PTSD—by showing the power of God and hope and how it has all pulled me through, and by showing that people can stand strong on their own two feet and overcome obstacles to become the person they want to be.

So as I said, I prayed for a sign, anything that would put me back behind that laptop and have me writing again with a purpose.

I woke up the next day, took a shower, and went downstairs like I did every day. I made it a habit in the mornings, while I was writing the book, to always go down the street to the local gas station to get coffee and these little Pillsbury mini cinnamon rolls that always seem to scream for me every time I walked in there. (No, I don't recommend a daily diet of this to those of you looking to lose weight; so as a trainer and nutritionist, please don't hold this against me or follow my example here.)

On this particular day, my anxiety was extremely high due to my apparent writer's block; and generally when anxiety would strike, it made me very nauseous, so the very last thing I wanted was coffee and food as I stood there in my kitchen. The way I was feeling slowed me down that morning, so my regular morning schedule was delayed just a little as I grabbed my laptop, set everything all up in the sunroom, and sat down much later than usual to start writing.

THE SHELF

I still wasn't feeling it, though. I paced the floors for about fifteen minutes. I didn't know where I was going to begin, but I just knew I needed to sit down and try the best I could with how I was feeling. However, before I sat down, I had a change of heart about the coffee and decided to just put my shoes on and go get some anyway. Sleep had been evading me for weeks, and I thought maybe the caffeine would help kick my writing brain into gear. So I got in my car and drove down the road to the gas station.

I did my thing as usual, got my coffee and cinnamon rolls, and got back into my car. As I got ready to pull out of the parking lot, I got a text from my friend Alison. Alison is also a devout Christian who has been a close friend of mine for many, many years. It just so happened that she was back in town, spending time with family before heading back to finish her military deployment overseas, and we had been talking for a couple of days while she was in town. She knew what was going on with me at the time and knew I was writing a book about my life. Her text asked me if I was listening to The Joy FM, the local Christian radio station here in the St. Louis area. I wasn't at the time, but I quickly pressed the button on my radio to change the station. "My Story" by Big Daddy Weave was playing.

Now, I hadn't talked to Alison at all about all the writing struggles I was having, I hadn't talked to Alison about all the prayers I'd been praying, and I hadn't talked to Alison about questioning if it was truly God's plan for me to tell my story. This text from her was sent unsolicited.

Over the years, Alison told me she often felt like God was calling her to pray for me or send me things; and when that happened, she would never hesitate to do so. Every time she had done it in the past, something was going on with me in my life where the prayers were really needed. It was a one-of-a-kind bond on a spiritual level that I didn't share with anyone else. And in this case, Alison had no idea that this was exactly the sign I was looking for.

Alison was meant to send me that text that day so I would hear that song. And ironically, if I hadn't been delayed in leaving to get my coffee, I would have never heard it. I was in my car for a total of two minutes; and in those two minutes, that song played. That song, along with Alison's words that followed, gave me the spark I needed to drive home and finish my book. She simply said, "This is you! This song is you!" God's hands were all over everything that day.

Later, I got into my car to go get my youngest daughter, Allison, from school. I don't normally pick her up, but her mom texted and asked me if I could that day; and of course, I did. So naturally, this was unplanned. As soon as I got in my car, the same song, "My Story," started playing again. I just sat there for a second, then looked up through my sunroof at the sky and said out loud, "Well played, big guy, well played." God drove the point home. My story needed to be told; my story had a purpose. And it was in that moment, listening to that amazing song, that I felt my story's purpose just might be what would help me find my own again.

"My Story"
Big Daddy Weave

If I told you my story
You would hear Hope that wouldn't let go
And if I told you my story
You would hear Love that never gave up
And if I told you my story
You would hear Life, but it wasn't mine

If I should speak then let it be
Of the grace that is greater than all my sin
Of when justice was served and where mercy wins
Of the kindness of Jesus that draws me in
Oh to tell you my story is to tell of Him

If I told you my story
You would hear victory over the enemy
And if I told you my story
You would hear freedom that was won for me
And if I told you my story
You would hear Life overcome the grave

THE SHELF

If I should speak then let it be
Of the grace that is greater than all my sin
Of when justice was served and where mercy wins
Of the kindness of Jesus that draws me in
Oh to tell you my story is to tell of Him

This is my story, this is my song
Praising my savior all the day long
This is my story, this is my song
Praising my savior all the day long
For the grace that is greater than all my sin
Of when justice was served and where mercy wins
Of the kindness of Jesus that draws me in
Oh to tell you my story is to tell

For the grace that is greater than all my sin
Of when justice was served and where mercy wins
Of the kindness of Jesus that draws me in
Oh to tell you my story is to tell of Him
Oh to tell you my story is to tell of Him

This is my story, this is my song
Praising my savior all the day long

"For the grace that is greater than all my sin." As I sat there in that moment, I reflected on everything. My story was full of sin; it was full of heartache, heartbreak, and struggle. But God had always forgiven me for my sins; His grace was always way more powerful than anything I ever did wrong. And not only did He forgive me, He always had led me to a better path; He always had equipped me with the tools I needed to become a better man and always provided me with everything necessary to live a better life, be happy, and make someone else happy too. Who was I to question anything He had done for me now after all that?

So I went back home that morning; and when I sat down with my laptop, my mind was finally clear again. My fingers started quickly moving across the keyboard; and suddenly, my author brain was back in the game. My prayers had been answered. Once again, God had surrounded me with the right people to help keep me on His path.

For I consider that the sufferings of this present time are not worth comparing with the glory that is to be revealed to us.

—Romans 8:18

CHAPTER 27

Losing Purpose

In the few years that followed, Misti and I were together on and off a few more times. I wish I could say that it was all easy for us after we were reunited; but again, not everyone lives happily ever after and ends up with the fairy tale ending you see on television.

We decided to take our relationship to the next level and move in together in the home she was renting following her divorce. I packed up my stuff from the lake house and was excited about what the future would hold for Misti and me.

We had our ups and downs for the better part of a year after that, and none of the struggles we had before seemed to go away even with our living together. I was struggling to find my purpose in life after retirement too, and that had a negative impact on me and everything I did at the time.

Despite how things ended, Misti and I had so many good times. We created so many amazing memories and did so many amazing things together. The good times were what always kept us going, despite our circumstances for almost six years. And no matter how hard things were sometimes, we did truly love each other. It was real, it was a special kind of love unlike any I had felt before, and it was the hardest thing in the world to feel that kind of love but know in my heart that we just weren't right for each other and that I had to let her go—hardest thing ever.

As I said, Misti and I had many good times and created so many amazing memories together, more than I could ever write about. She was my life; and for a long time, was the soul mate I thought I'd share the rest of my life with. As it turned out, things changed, and our many struggles took their toll. We both had faults, but neither of us was to blame for why it didn't work out. Regardless, there's so much more to our story than what you'll read here. We built years of memories—some good, some bad—and some of those times will always just stay between the two of us.

Soon after, I decided I was going to try to find a home to buy in Illinois. The home I found would end up being yet another example of God's continuing to do work on my life and guide me on the right path. The signs were everywhere. I saw some amazing photos of a beautiful home for sale on the internet. I loved the style of home and loved how it was set up. After looking through the photos, I went to the main page to discover that it was located on Faith Drive of all places. I looked at so many homes, both online and in person, over the course of a couple of months. None of them made me feel like how I felt when I walked inside this one. I thought maybe it was just another sign from God about where I was supposed to be; maybe this home was all part of His plan for me, so I made an offer; the owner countered; I accepted—done deal.

It was nice to own my own home and have my space just for me. It was perfect for me, and I was happy. But I was still on a mission to find myself during that time and was desperately trying to discover my purpose in life again, one that had really eluded me since retirement.

Eventually, I got to the point where I felt I had completely lost my purpose in life. I wasn't in a dark or bad place at all, and I didn't have any of those old feelings I had before about suicide. I lost my purpose and lost who I was, but I wasn't depressed about it. I didn't feel weak; I felt strong—strong enough to make some changes. I just knew I had to figure it out.

I wasn't feeling fulfilled at all and felt I needed to do something in my life to feel that way again, to find my purpose again. After raising three kids and retiring from the air force—a place where I always had people to take care of—I suddenly found myself sitting alone in my home day after day with nothing to do and no one to lead. I was starting to recognize it; I didn't like it. I was starting to miss people and my teams and my subordinates. I was starting to miss being responsible for teaching and helping others. I had tried so many different jobs and different things online after retirement, from real estate to working in marketing agencies. None of it was fulfilling me the way I wanted to feel fulfilled.

At the time, I felt I needed to do something different; I needed to go somewhere different. So one day, I decided to sell my vehicles, sell most of my things, and buy a truck that I could travel the United States in and live out of from time to time when I needed to. I was going to travel and find my purpose. I was going to travel and try to find a brand-new perspective on life that would help me find myself again.

I talked to people and bought books about different places in the states to visit. I thought long and hard about the experiences I could have and how they could positively influence me, give me new perspectives, and help shape my future. I was excited about the opportunity to see things I had never seen, do things I've never done, and experience things I've never experienced. In my mind, staying home in my bubble would've been the comfortable thing to do, and I felt that God wanted me to be uncomfortable. I was convinced that His plan was for me to travel, get uncomfortable outside my bubble, and go see a new world. I was convinced that this was His plan for me, and that I would find my purpose along the way.

I kept the traveling plan to myself for a while. However, because I was using social media to sell my things, people were noticing that things didn't seem quite normal with me, and some people started showing some concern. Of course, as I already said, it was never like that for me, but I started to understand why my actions were making people worried. So I decided it was time for me to finally let people know what I was planning to do.

I went "live" on Facebook and finally talked about my travel plans. I let everyone know that I wasn't crazy or upset, and that I was just excited about going on my journey and finding my purpose again. I never felt like it was a bad thing or a bad idea. To me, the ones who make decisions to go do something about their problems are the strong ones; the ones who just sit alone day after day are the weak ones. And in this moment and with this decision, I felt good; I felt strong. I felt like I was doing what I needed to do, to be happy with myself again.

Some people judged me for my decisions, thinking I was crazy, depressed, or suicidal. Other people understood. It was sad to find out how some people judged me negatively, and it was also sad to hear some of the cruel things people had to say about me. However, I wasn't going to let that faze me. It wasn't about anyone else; it was about me, my relationship with God, finding my purpose again, becoming who I knew in my heart I wanted to be but wasn't at the time—the person God knew I wanted to be. I was happy about my choices, excited about my journey, and just ready to do what I felt I was being led to do.

Over the next couple weeks, I posted about my trip often and posted a couple more videos talking about my travel plans. I found myself struggling with it all at times as I went back and forth about my decision and often caught myself questioning whether this was really what I was supposed to be doing. I try to keep my eyes open to what I feel God has planned for me in my life and follow the signs He provides. But many times in the past, I've misread signs and discovered that I only made some situations into what I wanted them to be.

THE SHELF

Deciphering between God's will and your own is hard sometimes when you try to live your life as a Christian, and my own free will and some of the decisions I've made because of it has always been my biggest challenge. It's been both a blessing and a curse. Most of the time, my problems were just me getting in my own way.

In one of my videos on Facebook, I talked about how I was struggling with my decision to take off and travel. At times, I was starting to wonder if the devil was at work and wanted me to flee from my issues instead of facing them. I went back and forth often during those couple weeks. I didn't want to misread signs; I didn't want to make a mistake.

Many people responded to my video and said they understood how I was feeling. A few others, whose opinions I valued greatly, felt that I needed to stay home and not run away. Even Misti saw this video, and while she would normally keep quiet about these things, she chose to respond to this post, further validating my thoughts about the trip being wrong and misguided. At the time, I didn't know what was right. But what I did know was that her response made a lot of sense to me at the time, as did the responses of many others.

In addition to that, I had just found out that my sister-in-law received an assignment to Scott Air Force Base—meaning, my brother and I would be together again. It was just another sign supporting the fact that I needed to stay home. (God's purpose for that reunion became very clear later too as you'll read in the last chapter of this book).

So with all that said, and since I was already having my own doubts about leaving, staying home is what I did. I decided I'd face whatever struggles I had head-on, and just try to make sense of them all from there.

And not long after I made that decision to stay, I felt God's presence again and started to feel I was now being led to serve in the ministry in some way, shape, or form. I even posted a video about having those feelings on Facebook. I had no idea what the feelings meant or what I would do. I certainly didn't have any aspirations of becoming a pastor or anything, but I had these strong feelings again, nonetheless. And after seeing God work after I had strong feelings like this in the past, I decided I had better just keep my eyes and ears wide open.

Misti ended up buying a home and closing on it during this time. We started talking again after she responded to my Facebook video. We still loved each other; and no matter how hard we tried, we just couldn't deny that. To make a long story short, I left my house and moved in with her in her new house. Things were okay with us at first; but shortly after I moved back, I knew it wasn't where I was supposed to be. I tried to be happy for months, but I just couldn't find it. And each day, God was tugging me in a different direction further and further away from Misti. Everyone already thought we were crazy to get back together again; everyone thought she was crazy for letting me go back and forth; everyone thought I was crazy to go back to her.

And as it turned out, everyone was right. I packed all of my things and left again once and for all to move back in to my home. This time was finally it. I just wasn't myself anymore, and it was time to let go and leave that life behind. I had to for myself and for her. It wasn't fair to her for me to keep going back and forth. I loved her so much, and I'm sure I always will. She was so hard to let go of. She was never to blame. Contrary to what we thought for many years, we just weren't meant to be; it just took me six years to finally figure it out. And as hard as it was to finally admit that to myself, I knew it was true.

I prayed on it often and felt God always pulling me away. I finally had to follow His lead and abandon my own wants and desires, and it would turn out that He had His reasons for making me feel the way He did. Now I just know in my heart that Misti and I are both in better places, and that we'll both be able to find our "happy" again one day.

> The LORD will fulfill his purpose for me;
> your steadfast love, O LORD, endures forever.
> Do not forsake the work of your hands.
>
> —Psalm 138:8

CHAPTER 28

The Glorious Unfolding

About a month before I left Misti for that last time, my brother Mark, sister-in-law Melissa, and niece Madison moved from Florida to Collinsville, Illinois, about fifteen minutes away from my house. It was an absolutely amazing time for all of us as we had spent so much time together already during our military careers, and Mark and I had always talked about how amazing it would be to retire together in the same place. Despite our childhood and being separated at young ages, God was not going to ever allow our bond to be broken—that was clear. What we wanted was actually happening now for us as adults, and God's hands were all over it.

Originally, Mark and I thought that he and his family would end up living close to me in O'Fallon, Illinois, after they arrived.

There was an amazing Christian school in O'Fallon for Madison, and living in a home in that area would be closer to me and a shorter drive for Melissa to the base each day. It just made good sense. But those were our thoughts, and God had very different ones.

Mark visited the school in O'Fallon and enjoyed the visit he had with them. The next day, he also had an appointment at Maryville Christian School in Maryville, Illinois. He was always thorough in his search for education for Madison. And as much as he liked O'Fallon and the convenience of the location, his visit with the school in Maryville was even better; and ultimately, that's where Madison would end up going to school. Mark felt something during his visit there and knew that was the right place for them to be.

As luck would have it that same day, Mark also found a nice big home near the school for rent. It all just worked out good for them. Again, Mark got a good feeling when visiting Maryville school; and as a Christian man himself, he went with what felt right and what felt was meant to be for Madison. Mark and Melissa have done such a great job raising an amazing kid, and they have always put her education and future first, no matter what they may have wanted for themselves. And in this case, the decision for her to attend Maryville Christian School ended up being a very good thing for all of us for many reasons.

The first thing Mark did after arriving in Illinois was look for a church. Maryville itself had a church; but after attending once, Mark and Melissa decided that it was just too big for them. They preferred a medium-sized church where there was a family and "everyone knows everyone" type of atmosphere. After doing some research of churches in their area, they found that Troy United Methodist Church—a medium-sized church—was minutes of their house. They attended service one Sunday and knew that was the place for them. It was what they were looking for; they had found their new church home.

Now on my end at the time, I had recently moved back into my home after leaving Misti, so I wasn't actively going to church and was, frankly, being lazy about checking out churches locally to see where my own new church home would be. Having lived in the area before, I knew of three different churches close to me that I had already attended, so I anticipated I'd probably just end up choosing one of those to attend on a regular basis. I just hadn't started going to any of them yet.

Football season started soon after Mark and Melissa arrived, and Mark and I took full advantage of the fact that we were now together again. Mark joined my fantasy football league—the same one I had been in for twenty years—and together, we had much to cheer about on Sundays. It became our thing; everything else that day took a back seat to that. No matter what was going on, we would be together watching the games on TV either at my house or his. It was pretty awesome.

More weeks than not, I would go to Mark's house to watch the games. Some Sundays I'd get there before they'd get home from church and be waiting for them when they got home. Again, I hadn't gotten into a church yet; and despite Mark's attempts to get me to go with them to their church, I just hadn't gotten around to doing it or deciding on what to do at that point. I knew in my heart that I needed to get into church again, though, as I had felt a little off and knew I had fallen a little off track in my faith. I had a lot on my mind after leaving Misti and moving back home; and at the time, my focus was more on other things going on in my life versus being focused on my relationship with God as it should've been.

One Sunday, I was at Mark's house waiting for him and Madison to get home from church. Shortly after I arrived, they both came busting through the door; Madison came to give me a hug as she did whenever she entered the room (more great perks having my family living close to me again). Mark and I were watching the game for about an hour after that when he remembered that the church pastor Andy had mentioned in service that day that they were hiring a new director of communications for Troy United Methodist Church. Mark told me about it and went on to say that the job description sounded so much like many of the things I had done in my career; and immediately after he heard Andy talk about it, he thought about me, my strengths, and thinking it might possibly be something I needed to look into.

Now, you have to understand that at this time, I had stopped sending out job applications and was really starting to just enjoy being fully retired. I could stay up as late as I wanted and sleep in as long as I wanted. I was getting used to it, so my desire to look for a job or actually find one was minimal. But after hearing about the job and taking all my previous feelings into consideration, I asked Mark for his laptop, wrote a cover letter, pulled my resume off of my

THE SHELF

e-mail account, and submitted my application for the Director of Communications position at the church. As soon as I did it, I told Mark that this would be the very last job application I would send out, and that if it was meant to be for me to work again, God would move some mountains to make things happen. And that's exactly what He did.

It was nearing the holidays, so the process took a couple of months, a couple of interviews, and a couple of meetings. I felt good about how the initial interview went, felt good about the "homework" I was asked to do and provide to them before and after that, and felt good about all the feedback I had received from the references I provided whom Pastor Andy talked to. There was no real pressure on me as I didn't necessarily need a job. But I still had those old feelings in the back of my mind that I would somehow end up serving in the ministry, so I had to continue on with the process, answer this call, and let whatever was meant to happen happen.

Thirty people applied for the director job. I was through most of the process when Pastor Andy called me to talk more and invite me to attend their next Sunday service. I remember thinking that I was likely out of the running for the job as I wasn't a member of the church yet and was certain that many of the other applicants probably were. At this point, I hadn't even attended a Sunday service, let alone become a member of the church, but I still wanted to follow through with things and go from there. I felt good about the conversation I had with Andy; he seemed sincere and interested in me. There was just something comfortable about that call; and despite not being a member, I hung up the phone thinking maybe there still was a chance—and maybe God was in the process of moving yet another mountain.

I had one more meeting with Pastor Andy and the church staff, this time a lunch meeting. During the lunch, it became increasingly clear that I was going to be their choice for the position. I didn't want to assume anything, but the context of the conversation and the comments in it were not things you say to someone whom you're about to break bad news to. Of course, nothing was official until I met with members of the church council; but as it turned out, two members of the council were going to be at the church after we finished lunch, and I was asked to go back with the staff to visit with them. They asked me a couple of questions, and one of the members left with Pastor Andy. A few minutes later, they returned, and it was then that I was officially offered the job.

I asked for a couple of days to think about it; and although I already knew I wanted the job, I just wanted to dig deeper on the Methodist church and make sure the church values and beliefs were in line with my own, so I could fully immerse myself in the job and communicate the vision and mission to people without hesitation. On *Shark Tank* (my favorite show), the investors are always telling people that they only like to invest in things that they truly believe in, and I'm the same way. It's a credibility thing, so I wanted to take a couple of days to really understand the Methodist way and make sure that I could live my life in a way that embraced their values while not compromising my own.

As it turned out, I soon discovered that I pretty much lived my life with Methodist values. The more I read, the more I knew I was in the right place. I was glad I took the time to learn more and see things for myself. I was glad that the church and its values were in line with my own; I really wanted them to be.

So as you can imagine, I was pretty overwhelmed about everything. So many mountains had to be moved in order for me to finally find my way. And while the road seemed very long and winding at times, keeping my focus in the right place always got me back on track. It's just amazing to look back at everything now from a different perspective, with a different set of eyes, and hindsight that's twenty-twenty. Because if just one of the amazing things that happened had been different, I would not be where I am today—my leaving Misti, Mark's moving to Illinois, Mark's choosing Maryville school, Mark's choosing Troy United Methodist Church, and our being together for football on Sundays.

I'm still at that job today. Sure, I don't get to sleep in anymore like I used to, but I have a purpose, and I know it's what I was meant to do. So many things have happened to make that crystal clear to me. God prepared me my whole life for this, from failing me out of the wrong air force job twenty-five years ago and putting me in the right one that would ultimately prepare me for this director position so many years later to bringing Mark and me back together again for good despite our childhood separation—so Mark could be the one to lead me in my faith and get me where God had always intended me to go.

Sometimes I really have to pinch myself to think that this is real life and not just some fairy tale. Because when you look back at it all, despite the ups and downs, my life really is a story of hope—and of sorrow, and of fear, and of triumph. It's a story of how a child could go through so much, yet still grow to be something he was told he never would be; and it's a story of how a man can end up so far down the wrong path, yet never lose hope, change, and ultimately find his way again. It's the stuff dreams and fairy tales are made of because God has that power, because He is that good, because He never abandoned me—because He never put me on the shelf.

CONCLUSION

Most people have a couple of moments in their life when things happen that they have no explanation for, the types of things that happen where they just can't put their finger on it as to why they did. I've been blessed to have lived an adult life where those moments have been plentiful. And as a true believer, I know that when I can't quite put my finger on something, it's likely that God is the one at work making them all happen—and to just go with it.

It's amazing how good life becomes when you can just learn to let go and do that. I've learned so much on my journey. I still have much more life to live and much more growing to do. Some days, I wish I could go back in time and change things. But knowing that God is always one step ahead, forging my path, I know that all my experiences—both good and bad—have been meant to be and have made me who I am today, and I'm okay with that.

I've learned to use my experiences to keep growing. I've learned to not let anything or anyone keep me from being the man I have always wanted to be. I've learned to forgive myself and not beat myself up so much anymore about the mistakes I've made. And I've learned that if I experience future moments of doubt or struggle, I just have to worry less and trust in the Lord to take care of me.

I'm thankful for the life I've lived and am truly blessed to have my faith and be able to put God first in my life now. With faith, anything is possible, as you've seen from all the magical things God has done in my life. I've been through a lot; but through God's grace and mercy, I'm now in a really good place and able to tell my story.

The past is over, and I'm committed now to a future with my eyes focused only on what's ahead. In doing that, I'm confident that I'll continue to grow and learn and experience many more amazing things. My life is not in the past; my life is in the future. And on days when I may doubt or question that, I'll just keep putting one foot in front of the other and keep in mind these amazing and profound words spoken by Dr. Martin Luther King Jr.: "If you can't fly then run, if you can't run then walk, if you can't walk then crawl, but whatever you do you have to keep moving forward."

It's time to move on and live my best life. It's time to live each day being led by Christ and living it with a happy and grateful heart. It's time to be selfless, serve God, and use my God-given gifts to lift up and help others. And it's time to finally let go of all my burdens and the past that no longer defines me.

> Therefore, if anyone is in Christ, he is a new creation; the old has gone, the new has come!
>
> —2 Corinthians 5:17

The end.

ABOUT THE AUTHOR

Dave DeRemer was born in Watertown, New York, and is a career marketer, communicator, speaker, and public relations expert. He is also a retired air force veteran of twenty-three years, a former professional bodybuilder and personal trainer, a father of three girls, and a loving grandfather.

He now enjoys his postmilitary life in the Midwest where he helps connect people to Jesus Christ every day as the Director of Communications for Troy United Methodist Church in Troy, Illinois.